# the six-figure freelancer

## YOUR ROADMAP TO SUCCESS IN THE GIG ECONOMY

## Laura Briggs

**AUTHOR OF** START YOUR OWN FREELANCE WRITING BUSINESS

Entrepreneur Press®

Entrepreneur Press, Publisher
Cover Design: Andrew Welyczko
Production and Composition: Eliot House Productions

This publication is designed to provide accurate and authoritative information
in regard to the subject matter covered. It is sold with the understanding that the
publisher is not engaged in rendering legal, accounting, or other professional services.
If legal advice or other expert assistance is required, the services of a competent
professional person should be sought.

Entrepreneur Press® is a registered trademark of Entrepreneur Media, Inc.

An application to register this book for cataloging has been submitted to the Library
of Congress.

ISBN 978-1-64201-116-6 (paperback) | ISBN 978-1-61308-439-7 (ebook)

Printed in the United States of America

25  24  23  22  21                                    10 9 8 7 6 5 4 3 2 1

# contents

# introduction

"Laura, your work samples are solid. But let me give you a piece of advice: You need to charge more. Your rate is so low that I'm not sure why you've set it there. It makes me question the value."

It was 2013. I'd just left my job to officially become a full-time freelancer. I'd taken a call with a prospective freelance writing client while sitting in my car, but the conversation left me confused.

I'd had plenty of clients who said I was too expensive and that they could get better prices elsewhere. But no one had ever told me I charged too little before.

The encounter caused a sea change in the way I approached my freelance business. The truth was that I couldn't compete with every other freelancer out there on price alone. That was a surefire way to race to the bottom. And, as I'd just discovered, it was driving some great clients away because they assumed my low prices reflected some problem in the process. Maybe they thought I delivered late or copied someone else's work, but none of those details mattered. I'd accidentally branded myself as "cheap."

A few days later, one of my best clients told me it would be easiest if I just took over all his blogging projects for him. He needed four blog posts a week and didn't want to schedule them on social media, enter them into his online content management system, or track keywords on his own. Having previously sold my blog posts only in batches of four to ten at a time, The client wasn't just asking me for the core blog posts, but add-ons that could increase the total value of this contract. This introduced me to the concept of both retainers (ongoing work) and upsells (additional services.) It was time to let go of the idea that my business could thrive on a project-by-project basis. It was time to raise my prices, convert as many clients as possible to retainers, and look for other opportunities to scale my business. It was time to work toward becoming a six-figure freelancer.

## The Road to Six Figures

Freelancing is definitely having a moment, and in the coming decades the influence of independent contractors will be felt clearly in economies around the world. Technology has made it easier to work from home, and the remote work revolution means that more companies are recognizing that it's best to partner with the most qualified talent, no matter where that person lives. Given the recent impact of a worldwide pandemic and the greater need for and interest in remote work, freelancing is front and center now more than ever.

I started freelancing in 2012 as a side hustle. I was working during the day and going to graduate school at night. My plans of working in education had been shattered after just one year teaching middle school in Baltimore City. I was lucky enough to get an offer to work in marketing, which I took while I figured out what to do with my life. During that time, I inventoried every skill I thought I might have and landed on writing as a skill set I could expand on to make extra money. In my day job, the company ended up using some of my slogans and marketing tag lines in national campaigns, so I started to research marketing, advertising, and content strategy.

Before long, I was earning a few hundred dollars a month for freelance writing I completed before work, at night, and on the weekends. But I was terrified to leave my day job. I didn't know if I'd be able to make enough money on my own, month in and month out. As it turned out, however, using that side hustle as my launchpad was an extremely successful strategy and one I would recommend rather than trying to jump feet first into a freelance business without a safety net.

I stopped working at my day job 13 months after I started side hustling. My revenues grew dramatically when I began dedicating 40 hours per week, rather than 10 to 15, into completing work and looking for new projects. I've been able to sustain or grow my freelance business every year since 2014 as a six-figure enterprise, topping $200,000 for the first time in 2018.

Over the years, I've met many other freelancers who also scaled their businesses to an advanced level. Many of them are featured throughout this book so you can benefit from their expertise and tips on growing your business, whether you're a bookkeeper, virtual assistant (VA), web designer, writer, or any other kind of freelance creative service provider. But I've also met many people who struggled to surpass $3,000 to $5,000 a month, often toiling more than 50 hours a week to crank out projects as quickly as possible.

That's why I wrote this book, which is for freelancers of all stripes who already have an existing business and are looking to scale to the next level. Because whether you're looking for the road map to scale your business the right way or you're one of those freelancers stuck on the hamster wheel, making too little money for far too much time and energy, this book is designed to help you analyze and tweak your business model so you can earn a good living being paid what you're worth as a freelancer in your chosen industry.

For some freelancers reading this book, success might look like $80,000 in revenue. For others, it will be well over the $100,000 mark.

No matter your financial goal, the end result is the same: owning and operating a fulfilling, service-based business that meets or exceeds client expectations and allows you to live the life you want.

## What to Expect in This Book

Here's what you can expect in this book: a chapter-by-chapter breakdown of the most important elements of a high-level freelance business. You'll discover how to achieve the mindset you need to be successful, how to decide whether to run your business as a solopreneur or as an agency owner, how to connect with the right clients on the right projects, how to optimize your business model, and how to continue growing even after you reach your desired revenue goals.

You'll find numerous references to resources throughout this book. To make things easy and to ensure they're updated when those resources reference technology or other time-sensitive information, you can find them in PDF format on the book's website, www.sixfigurefreelancebook.com, which you'll always have access to as a buyer of this book. These resources and worksheets will help you complete the necessary exercises to analyze and implement road map suggestions in your own freelance business. In addition to the resources called out in the book, you'll find bonus material, like scripts you can use for awkward conversations with clients and subcontractors and invoicing software for freelancers, at www.sixfigurefreelancebook.com/resources.

Even though there are many references to the six-figure mark in this book, adjust accordingly as you read if your financial goals are under $100,000. There is no wrong answer in terms of what your next-level vision of your freelance business should be. If your sweet spot is $50,000 a year, this book will still help you get the most out of your working time and make sure you have the right clients, systems, and support to thrive.

A quick note: I'm a freelance writer, but that doesn't mean the tips in this book will only apply to someone with a copywriting business. I've included numerous examples of how these strategies might apply to someone who is freelancing other tasks, and have shared the wisdom of 19 other six-figure freelancers to help you see how they work for them, too!

Your toolkit is here. There's no reason not to move forward. Now is the time for you to level up your freelance business to benefit yourself, your clients, and the people most important to you. Let's get to work!

# your freelance launch point

For many years, freelancing hasn't been taken seriously by the traditional education or employment market. There are plenty of articles that discuss the dangers of freelancing. In 2017, with the exception of my own alma maters, multiple college professors declined to have me speak to their classes about the opportunities available in freelancing. One even told me, "We prefer to prepare students for real careers."

The perception that freelancing is just a temporary source of cash for broke creatives, that it's so highly unstable it's not worth pursuing, and that it's for low-paid service providers is a myth. But then there's the other end of the spectrum: the ads promising you a mai tai on the beach while you type, earning millions by working an hour a day. The truth is somewhere in the middle.

Technology and the demand for online marketing have completely changed the freelancing game. The need for online marketing in the form of websites, advertising, apps, social media material, blogs, and more have created new markets for creatives to get work and make more money. A 2018 study by MBO Partners found that one in five full-time freelancers was already generating six figures in revenue in their business, up from one in eight in 2011. In this chapter, we'll dive deeper into some of the numbers that show where you currently stand in your freelance business, so that you know your starting point and can create realistic and measurable goals going forward.

As an existing freelancer, you have already done some of the legwork to establish yourself as a business owner. You have a proven business model because you're already converting and selling clients into your service. But how consistent that is or how much money it brings in might be the metrics you want to improve. This book is not geared for beginners, but rather to help existing freelancers who aspire to that six-figure plateau.

While every freelance business is unique because of the services provided and the approach of the individual freelancer, freelancers often face a few common issues that block growth. These have to do with their revenue, their clients, and their overall vision and strategy.

Often the pathway to generating more revenue appears naturally as you address each of the challenges listed above. Let's look at them one by one.

## Aiming for Six Figures as a Freelancer

Six figures in revenue for your freelance business breaks down to just over $8,333 per month. Since some months will always be better than others, it's helpful to focus on a slightly higher round number, like $8,500 or $9,000, so that you have some wiggle room.

Increasingly, six figures a year is becoming the new barometer for the desired full-time freelance revenue in the U.S.—especially if you have debts to pay. If you went to college, you're likely dealing with the added pressure of student loan debt. In 2020, the average student loan debt of a four-year college graduate in the United States was just over $32,000.

That said, remember that revenue is what your business brings in, but not necessarily what you keep. Your business will need to pay out some expenses (like a virtual assistant, software, job board fees, or website hosting), in addition to paying taxes. So if you're aiming for six figures in *income* rather than *revenue*, you'll need to push your monthly revenue goals even higher, such as $12,000 or more.

If your business doesn't bring in six figures yet but does generate consistent revenue for you, either as a side hustle or full-time work, congratulations! This is a feat in and of itself, given how many people struggle with the feast-or-famine cycle common in the gig economy.

You should be equally proud of breaking $70K to $90K in revenue if your previous numbers were below $60K. Even if you don't crush that six-figure goal this year, growth is the most important metric. And you can't measure growth if you don't know where you're beginning.

No freelancer can grow their business without knowing their starting point. This launch point is crucial to developing the right money mindset and can also help open your eyes about how you are truly spending your time by adding up the hours you dedicate to your business each week, including core activities like marketing and client projects.

Even experienced freelancers face many different challenges. One of the most common is how to break the feast-or-famine cycle. Many freelancers find themselves trapped in this pattern, where they have no work for weeks or even months at a time and then suddenly have so much to do they can barely meet all their deadlines. One of the tasks we'll tackle in building this road map and strategy guide is to build in more recurring and consistent revenue for you.

Figuring out your starting point will allow you to more reliably predict cash flow for your business. This is helpful not just for knowing the amount of money you're bringing in, but also for allowing you to make important decisions about key investments you will need as you grow your business, such as hiring a virtual assistant.

## *What's Your Starting Point?*

You can start by getting familiar with your numbers now.

Figure 1–1 below shows you some categories to consider when determining your starting point. If you want a guided exercise for determining your starting point, you can find the companion worksheet (Handout #1) and the Six-Figure Freelancer Scorecard (Exercise #1) for this chapter at www.sixfigurefreelancebook.com/resources to help you

---

### Your Six-Figure Freelance Starting Point

1. How much money did your freelance business generate last year? _____

   _____

2. What was your average monthly revenue? _____

   _____

3. What's your next monthly revenue goal, based on a meaningful but not overwhelming improvement? _____

   _____

4. How many clients do you currently have? _____

   _____

5. How many hours per week do you log? _____

   _____

6. What is your average revenue per client? _____

   _____

7. What is your effective hourly rate? _____

   _____

---

*Figure 1-1.* STARTING POINT WORKSHEET

figure out where your business needs the most work. The Six-Figure Freelancer Scorecard will help you step back to see your business from a 30,000-foot view covering many of the most important topics in this book. By taking the Scorecard, you'll get a better sense of where to direct your attention with chapters in the book and where your business has the most room for improvement. Then you can use this book to help you with those areas.

Take a look at your last year of earnings, if you have that information. If you've only been in business for six months, look at your monthly revenue over that time period. If your revenue has been fluctuating, it's helpful to know both your monthly revenue and average monthly revenue. Average monthly revenue is easier to work with because it helps balance out your slow seasons or that month you took a two-week vacation. Get your average by adding the number of months you've been working and your total revenue during that time period, and then divide the total revenue by the number of months you've been working. If you're trying to learn your average monthly revenue for last year, take your total annual revenue and divide by 12.

That number is your starting point. You might be excited about it if your business has been relatively consistent or if you started from zero and are now regularly earning $3,000 per month.

But if you arrive at a number that doesn't get you excited, remember that this is just the beginning. You're building a road map and strategy based on those results, but it's not your endgame.

When you look at your monthly or average monthly revenue, how does it make you feel? Did the number surprise you? Does it feel far off from the $8,000 to $10,000 you're hoping to bring in as you scale? Don't worry—knowing your number helps you figure out how much distance there is between where you've been and where you want to go. Record this number in a spreadsheet or post it on a corkboard next to your desk using a graph and pushpin, and use a piece of string to track your rising revenue as you work through this book over the coming months. You can even draw a graph on a whiteboard. Having this visual reminder and a place to record your data constantly keeps you in check and reminds you of your goals.

## Setting Realistic Financial Goals for Your Freelance Business: Your Finances

Now that you know your starting point, it is time to begin developing a goal for your monthly freelance revenue in the future. There are two mistakes you want to avoid when determining this number. The first is setting a goal that is far too low to keep you motivated. The second is setting a goal that is much higher than your current consistent revenue. By putting too much pressure on yourself, you can set yourself up for failure and make it difficult to feel that your goal is achievable.

Here's an example of each scenario. Let's say your current monthly freelance revenue is $1,500. If you set a monthly goal of $1,700, that is not enough of an increase. In fact, you can achieve this higher number with just one more client or even one small piece of a project. Instead, a more realistic goal might be $2,000 or $2,500 a month. These are a stretch from where you are currently, but they are also within reach, given the current success of your freelancing business.

Likewise, if you're currently bringing in $1,500 a month, setting an immediate goal of $8,500 a month is a significant stretch. Some people might be able to reach this in a few months, but if you're a highly self-critical person, you'll feel like a failure after just one month if you don't bring in another $7,000. Instead, approach it more realistically. One of the most powerful things you can do for your freelance business is to focus on a series of small, stackable wins. Your first monthly goal might be $2,000, which is within reach from your $1,500 set point, but is enough of a boost for you to feel confident about raising your rates while pitching new clients.

I often recommend to coaching clients that they work on hitting their new monthly revenue goal for two or three months in a row before scaling, but if you're starting off at a relatively low number, you might move up incrementally each month instead. Once you have your first $2,500 month, you might be ready to push to $3,000 a month. The bigger the jump between where you're at and where you intend to be, the more important it is to stick to your goal for two to three months at a time before increasing it.

Let's see how these sudden revenue jumps can be challenging for a freelancer. Take John, an experienced freelance web developer who's currently bringing in $3,000 a month. On his path to hitting the six-figure mark, his first revenue goal might be $5,000 a month. This is within reach for his current revenue level, but it also pushes him to complete more pitches and sales calls to bring in one or two more projects.

If John were to hit his $5,000 goal within two months and then immediately push his goal to $10,000 a month, this might be difficult because he has not yet adjusted his schedule, workflow, and marketing to the new demands of his business. Every time you increase your revenue, you have to be very careful about the clients in your roster and whether you have the systems, strategies, and people to support you with that new revenue and workload.

Now imagine that John has four $5,000 months in a row. He has identified some of the gaps in his business and taken additional steps to find support, such as hiring a coach, investing in new onboarding software, and hiring his first virtual assistant. Now that he has these additional strategies and structure in place, setting a goal of $8,000 or $10,000 a month is much more achievable.

He has made adjustments to help support the work he needs to increase his revenue and freed up his time, thanks to software and team members. If John had scaled to $10,000 a month immediately, however, he would have lacked that support, leaving him burned out, overwhelmed, and frustrated.

He might assume that this burnout is tied to the fact that he had a much bigger month financially. This would detract from his excitement at having achieved his financial goal and might even force him to downsize his business because of the perceived stress. But John's problems weren't from operating at the $10,000 level—it's because he was attempting to operate at the $10,000 level without the necessary tools in place to support him.

Working with freelancers one-on-one has shown me that it is often easier than you expect to scale your freelance revenue. Where most people fall short, however, is in making sure that they have brought the right clients on board at this new revenue level and have evaluated the client's business for potential gaps to help the client succeed.

You can see now why it is so important to know your starting point, so that you can choose realistic goals for your next couple of months. If you're currently bringing in $1,000 a month, it might take you some time to get to the $8,000-a-month mark. Don't worry about it. One of the most overlooked aspects of building a successful business is the importance of making consistent, gradual changes to your goals, workflow, and resources. Mapping out a few months of goals could show you how you could go from $1,000 to $3,000 to $5,000 to $8,000 a month relatively quickly.

## What Got You Here Might Not Get You There: Your Clients

It is possible to build a six-figure freelancing business with the wrong clients. In fact, this happens often. Building a roster of low-paying, frustrating clients often leads people who hit the six-figure mark for the first time to get burned out and take three months off—or even quit altogether.

To get a sense of where you're at with your current client lineup, complete that section of the companion worksheet (seen in Figure 1–2 on page 9), which you can get for free at www.sixfigurefreelancebook.com/resources. If you prefer the printable version that you can return to every few months and fill out again, download the PDF online.

One of the most important things to recognize about building a six-figure freelancing business is that it requires careful evaluation of your clients to choose the right ones. It is very common for new freelancers to take on any client who throws them a paying project. It can be so exciting to land new clients that it doesn't even register with many freelancers that they should be selective. Many of them might be approaching freelancing as their side hustle and are simply excited about the opportunity, but others might be looking to hit particular financial goals and will take on any client, no matter who it is.

Running an advanced freelance business means you have to know exactly who you do and don't want to work with. It's very possible that

## Client Lineup Worksheet

| | |
|---|---|
| How much money did your freelance business generate last year? | |
| What is your average monthly revenue? | |
| What's your next monthly revenue goal, based on a meaningful but not overwhelming improvement? | |
| How many clients do you currently have? | |
| What is your average revenue per client? | |
| Are all these clients on relatively equal terms based on: | |
| Quality of projects | |
| Amount of time spent in communication or edit mode | |
| Payment | |
| Ease of receiving payment | |
| How many hours per week are you working? | |
| Do you want the number of hours you're working per week to change? | |
| Who else is on your team supporting you? Junior freelancers, VAs, other experts? | |
| What's your effective hourly rate? Your effective hourly rate is the total of all revenue for the year divided by all of the hours that you worked. | |
| How would you score yourself as far as taking days off and vacations? (1 = no days off; 10 = take regular days off and vacations) | |
| Do you feel like you're working with too many individual clients at a time? | |

*Figure 1-2.* CLIENT LINEUP WORKSHEET

some of the clients on your current roster are not the right fit for your business's new model. Price alone is not the only reason to consider letting a client go—their communication style, the quality and size of their project, and how well it fits into your business model are all important factors.

Here are some questions you should consider as you evaluate your current client roster:

$ In seeing each client's name, do I feel excited or energized about the work I do for them?

$ Are there any clients who make me roll my eyes or get frustrated, not because of the work, but because of their personalities?

$ Is there anyone who requires a lot of work for very little pay?

$ Is there anyone who has a project or scope size so big that I regularly feel overwhelmed?

$ Is there anyone who doesn't pay on time, doesn't give me the direction I need to be successful, or requests too many edits?

$ Is there anyone with small projects that aren't worth the time I have to invest in getting up to speed on their client requests, branding, or guidelines?

As you work through these questions, you might start to notice there are some clients you don't enjoy working with, are too much hassle, or don't pay enough. These should be the first clients you aim to replace. If you don't have a consistent client roster yet, file these issues away to watch out for as you bring on new clients. You'll want to come back to these questions regularly as your client roster grows to make sure you are working with the right people.

One key to running a successful and consistent six-figure freelancing business is being mindful of who you allow into your world. Building a freelance business with the wrong clients is setting yourself up for failure. To hit that six-figure mark, you might even need to fire a client and leave money on the table. You'll learn more about client management in Chapter 4.

The important thing to remember is that you don't need to judge yourself for who you're working with now. Running a successful business is an achievement, even if you haven't yet hit your revenue goals. Remember that many small businesses close after the first few years. Of companies that started in 2014, for example, only 56 percent made it to their fifth year. The very fact that you picked up this book shows you want to take the next step toward fine-tuning your company.

To do that, though, you must be honest. Finding all the gaps in your current schedule is necessary to set the tone with the next version of your business—one that is more efficient, effective, and profitable.

There's a lot more on clients in Chapter 4. For now, you want to have a general sense of who might not be the right fit. Keep that in the back of your mind for future chapters.

## Are Your Old Habits No Longer Serving You?

Choosing a strong client base is one step toward scaling your business. Another is your willingness to let go of old habits that no longer serve your goals. This is the first step of adopting a better business owner mindset. We'll go into more details about mindset in the next chapter, but let's talk briefly about how you can become more aware of any habits that might need to change.

Running a six-figure freelance business requires vision, focus, and strategy. For many aspiring six-figure freelancers, a lot of hard work got them to the point of earning $50,000 or $80,000. If you built your business by putting in 60 hours a week or working with exhausting clients, you might be afraid that the only way to generate more revenue is to take on even more hours and more difficult clients.

If this means spending more time at the computer, accompanied by eyestrain, carpal tunnel, or burnout, you might just decide not to build your business any further.

Here are some of the most common bad habits that might have "worked" until this point, but no longer allow room for growth in your freelance business:

$ Working with low-paying, frustrating, or time-consuming clients
$ Taking on too many one-time projects that have no potential to grow into retainers or long-term relationships

$ Marketing too little and risking the loss of one or two key clients, that would bring your revenue to $0

$ Working with 10 to 12 clients at a time across multiple niches or project types, making you feel like you're juggling way too much at once

$ Working only with one client who has taken over all your time, leaving you to sell dollars for hours

$ Assuming that because handling everything on your own worked up till now that you can't give up control over any part of your business, even to a qualified virtual assistant

$ Believing that you can't run a six-figure business, either as an agency owner or by yourself

$ Not knowing how to financially plan for your six-figure business and therefore ignoring important implications for your liability and tax exposure

$ Failing to consider yourself an "expert" and continuing to charge the same prices you did when you started

$ Taking on projects outside your interest level or expertise because you need the money

This is not an all-inclusive list. But it's clear that what it takes to push through to the next revenue level is a combination of mindset and strategy. Both elements must be in place to succeed. All too often, freelancers are looking for a magic bullet: strategies they can implement quickly and easily.

But if you have a mindset issue around, say, your fear of sales calls, that gremlin will crop up every time you need to schedule or show up to a sales call. No amount of strategy and planning will compensate for a mindset issue like that; you must be willing to take a step back and figure out how to reframe that fear. We'll talk more about this in Chapter 2.

## Avoiding Burnout: Your Schedule and Systems

As a business owner, it can be hard to turn off your brain. You're probably thinking about your business and your clients around the clock, scribbling down notes on your grocery list or making a to-do list on your phone when you're out and about.

One of the biggest challenges faced by freelancers is figuring out how to structure your day so you don't burn out.

When you work a regular job, your workday typically has set hours, like 9 to 5. When you physically report to work each morning and leave each day, it's easy to draw a firm boundary between your work life and your home life. But what about when you work for yourself and your "office" is anywhere you have access to your laptop?

You might not even realize how many hours you're logging for your business. And if you're quoting your projects on a per-piece basis, you might be spending more time than you know communicating with clients, doing research, and making edits—not to mention keeping up with the administrative work, pitching, and all the other back-end details of your business.

The goal is not to eliminate that excess work entirely. It's to become aware of it, make a plan to reduce the time you spend on it, and optimize each and every one of your billable hours for clients.

To do this and build a road map to the next step, it's time to figure out what tasks you're currently doing in your business and how long they're taking you.

For one week, keep track of everything you do for your business. That includes brainstorming, taking notes, sending emails, posting on social media, and more. If you don't want to write it down on paper, use a tool like Toggl. Toggl has both a mobile app and a website that are linked, and offers a timer that you can click on and off when you're working on multiple projects. I love Toggl for tracking time on client work vs. marketing or business building, so you can add different tags for your projects if you want.

For most freelancers, that work breaks down into several different categories:

$ *Active marketing*: Pitching, connecting with people on LinkedIn, writing emails, visiting job boards, following up with past proposals and pitches
$ *Client work*: Researching, creating, updating/editing, and finalizing
$ *Communication*: With team members, clients, or other professionals

$ *Administrative tasks*: Creating contracts, invoices, proposals, and more
$ *Learning*: Watching videos, reading books, listening to podcasts, or taking online courses

There will always be both communication and marketing aspects to running your business. But keep in mind that they shouldn't be taking up the bulk of your time. If you already have a proven service with great results, your marketing should only make up around 20 percent of your time. You already know what marketing channels convert well for you, and you can dial into these while occasionally testing new concepts. The same goes for communicating with your clients. Administrative time might vary from week to week, but can usually be grouped together across two half-days with a streamlined system.

While the learning component is not necessary every week, freelancers are far more likely than typical employees to invest in their skills to stay on the leading edge of their industry. Since so many freelancers work in digital and creative spaces, it's important to keep tabs on what's working, what isn't, and the newest tools you can use to run your company more efficiently and deliver better results for your clients.

But before we create a plan to tackle those, track your time for one week.

I recommend setting up Toggl (or whichever system you choose, whether it's a simple spreadsheet or a spiral notebook) to reflect the five categories above. If there's something else that takes up a significant amount of time in your freelance business, include it as a separate category.

For the next week, track your time every time you're working. Toggl has both a desktop and a mobile app, so even if you're on a phone call, it should be easy to set the timer.

If you don't want to track using Toggl, another tool that can really help you see how you're spending your day is RescueTime. There's a 14-day free trial, which should be enough for what we're doing here, but if you find it useful you can always pay to continue using the software.

RescueTime alerted me to the fact that I was spending 12 hours a week doing email a few years ago. That was a wakeup call—there's no need to spend that much time dealing with your inbox, especially if that time could be better directed to marketing or client delivery. Be aware that RescueTime will flag your social media time, too, which is often a big time waster for people!

Once you're done tracking your time for a week, look at the results critically and ask the following questions:

- $ Is there anything that surprised me in terms of how much time I spend on it?
- $ Did my tracking highlight any unproductive habits or activities that don't really move me or my business forward?
- $ Do I spend time on any tasks that don't require my expertise and might be better suited to a virtual assistant or other contractor?

Highlight some of the activities you want to return to as you go through the book and adjust your schedule.

### Determining Your Fully Booked Point

"Fully booked" looks different from one freelancer to another. And yes, it is still possible to run a part-time freelance business that generates a high revenue level (I've done it twice and am doing it as I write this book!).

For one freelancer, fully booked is 40 hours per week, split between client projects and other work, like marketing and admin. For another, they're happy at 25 hours a week because that allows them to remain fresh for client work while exploring other pursuits. Not everyone enjoys the constant hustle of running a business.

Don't assume that scaling up your business means scaling up your hours accordingly. There have been many studies showing that simply logging more hours—especially if you're pushing yourself beyond 40 or 50 hours per week—decreases productivity. It also increases the chances of burnout. While you might be able to keep up with an accelerated schedule for a little while, it will eventually drain you and leave you less able to handle even a part-time schedule after this heavy lifting period. It's much better to choose a realistic goal for the amount of time you'll spend working each week.

### *Creating Your Ideal Week: An Important Exercise*

Now that you've probably spotted some of the gaps in your current schedule, your eyes might be open to a better way of doing things.

Whether you map this out by hand or use an extra calendar in Google, set up an ideal workweek for your business. Perhaps you noticed in the time-tracking exercise that you spend too much time on administrative tasks and email. Use that information to set a new weekly cap to help you manage your time better.

For example, if you previously spent ten hours per week on your email, perhaps your first order of business is cutting that down to five. That's one hour per workday, or a chance to check your email once in the morning and once in the afternoon. In your ideal calendar, set up time blocks to do this.

You can easily make a whole new calendar inside Google or set one up inside Toggl. When I add tags, such as "Work on Novel," inside Toggl, I'm aiming to hit a specific goal per week, like five hours. When I'm trying to stay out of my email inbox, though, I include a cap in the tag, like "Email Checking—Max 3 Hours." This serves as an extra reminder that while I may not hit that goal every week, I should still be aware of those rabbit holes where I can get distracted by unproductive tasks or busywork like email.

As you dive into future chapters, you'll learn more about some of the tips and strategies I recommend when streamlining your freelance business to cut out what doesn't matter and add in more of what does.

This chapter has focused heavily on the financial and systems components of your business. But how you feel about your work and the way it connects to your life's purpose is a huge part of the bigger picture that can't be neglected. In Chapter 2, you'll learn more about the vision and mindset components of running a freelance business that's destined for next-level greatness.

— CHAPTER SUMMARY POINTS —

$ Your clients, your finances, your systems, and your mindset all play a role in how you perform in your business.

$ Address and manage the good and bad habits you currently rely on in your business. Before you can design a plan for where you want to go, get real with the numbers in your business so you can set realistic, forward-facing goals.

## *Resources Mentioned in This Chapter*

The resources listed below can all be found at www.sixfigurefreelancebook.com/resources.

$ Six-Figure Freelance Launch Point, Handout #1

$ Six-Figure Freelancer Scorecard, Exercise #1

# master your mindset

D o you ever take a step back to think about your business goals? Or are you stuck in the day-to-day grind of marketing, completing client projects, and sending out invoices? Scaling your business means taking the time not just to work *in* your business but also to work *on* it—and to work on your mindset. Mindset work is an important part of framing how and why you do what you do. It also helps to ensure that you carve out the time to envision your future.

If you're like I was a few years ago, you may be tempted to skip this chapter and get into what you see as "the good stuff." But the mindset work *is* the good stuff. In fact, your limiting beliefs and fears might be the only thing holding you back from a truly successful business. I know that was the case for me. For years I brushed off "mindset work" as something ridiculous that Tony Robbins charged thousands of dollars for while other business owners focused on serving clients as completing projects.

Little did I know, however, that there were a lot of limiting beliefs inside my head that were subconsciously keeping me treading water with the wrong clients.

Up to that point, my freelance business had been earning $9,000 to $12,000 per month for more than a year. While this was certainly a significant accomplishment in terms of growth from where I started (earning $1,200 in my first full month of freelancing as a side hustle!), I was frustrated that no matter what I tried, I couldn't break past that $12,000 limit.

Then I started taking my mindset work seriously and sought to uncover some of the nasty beliefs I'd accidentally internalized as truths. It was only then that I was able to open the floodgates to a more productive business model. I hit my first $20,000 month and never looked back. In this chapter, you'll learn what a mindset practice looks like and how to start using it to your advantage.

Everyone's journey to a better mindset will be different. Regularly looking for and identifying those baked-in subconscious thoughts that might be blocking you from growing your company will unlock new levels of happiness, awareness, and prosperity.

## What's Your "Why"?

If you don't have an underlying motivation to build and scale your business, working on client projects and doing the marketing to keep your revenue flowing starts to feel a lot like running on a hamster wheel. But if you identify that "why," you will have a north star to guide your efforts.

Your "why" informs every aspect of how you perform in your business. It's what you fall back on when you hit a roadblock or have a bad day. So long as the passion and interest are there, there are always ways to tweak or systematize your business to make it work more effectively for you.

Six-figure freelancer Cyn Balog, a ghostwriter and novelist, said she always keeps her passion front and center and revisits it often to make sure it still fits where her business is headed.

She noted: "If you want it bad enough, you can make it work. I told myself before I quit that if I had to, I'd do anything to make my freelancing career work—take unsavory jobs, work on nonfiction positions, apply for anything I could. I never had to do any of that, but it's my safety net. Because the truth is, the worst assignment in the world is still better than that full-time job I used to have. I take time just to be thankful every day that I made the change, because not a day goes by that I don't wish I'd done it sooner!"

Much like Cyn, I often ask myself when I'm having a bad day if it's as rough as any of the days I had as a middle school teacher. I also keep the vision of where I want my business to go and who I want to affect in mind to remind myself of my "why," just as Cyn does.

Your "why" might be in the list below or it might be something you come up with on your own:

> "Know why you started your business in the first place. Having that front of mind will make all the decisions you have to make on a daily basis so much easier."
>
> –Jason Resnick, freelance behavioral marketing and automation specialist

$ I want the freedom to decide who I work with, when I work, and how I do it.

$ I want to build my freelance career to retire my partner from having to work anymore or to give us more financial freedom.

$ I want to pay down debts or save up for something special.

$ I want to help business owners achieve XYZ with my freelance services.

$ I want to wake up every day excited to work on the projects I'm most passionate about.

$ I want to have the flexibility to work from home and spend more time with my family.

$ I want to create my own opportunities by learning new things and setting rates I feel excited about charging.

One of my big "whys" was that I wanted to work only with clients I liked and respected and build a career that would support me through multiple moves required by my husband's military career.

Once you have your "why" firmly set—and preferably written down somewhere—it's time to think about whether you have any beliefs that are making it hard for you to connect your motivation to the practices and habits you need to adopt for your business to grow. These are known as *limiting beliefs*, and they're not always easy to recognize. In the next section, you'll learn how to spot sneaky limiting beliefs I have identified and what to do about them.

## How to Recognize Limiting Beliefs

The next step in mastering your mindset is to become aware of your limiting beliefs. A limiting belief is a concept that's wired into your brain and accepted as real, but not necessarily true. You can have limiting beliefs about yourself, other people, or the world. You might openly acknowledge them as true, or they might be buried so deeply in your subconscious that you can only discover them by doing mindset work. Both types are potentially harmful, shutting you off from new opportunities and keeping you stuck in a pattern that prevents you from building the freelance business you want.

It's important to recognize that we all have limiting beliefs. Most people don't think they have any because they think *their* limiting beliefs are true. Family members, friends, teachers, coaches, culture, and society can all contribute to your limiting belief system.

These beliefs often start small, like a teacher who repeatedly tells you to pay attention or calls your parents in to talk about how you distract other students. Eventually, you can internalize this message as "I'm a very distracted and unfocused person. I need to watch that about myself, and I'll really struggle with any project that requires my full attention."

Especially when these limiting beliefs begin in childhood, the habit that caught someone else's attention might no longer exist or could have been blown out of proportion. But the damage is done, and you have catalogued that belief as true.

There are many different kinds of limiting beliefs, and how they affect people will vary from one person to another. These limiting beliefs can be very specific or general.

Some of the most common examples of limiting beliefs include:

$ "I am not (tall/smart/funny/etc.) enough to get what I want."

$ "I don't deserve to have _____."

$ "I don't want other people to think I am (greedy/self-centered/ aggressive/etc.)."

$ "I just can't handle _____."

$ "I'm destined to fail, so it's not even worth trying."

$ "I don't have enough time/energy/ experience/money."

$ "There's not enough _____ for everyone, so I'm being greedy by taking more than my fair share."

$ "There's something really wrong with me and I need to be fixed."

If any of the above limiting beliefs resonated with you or you think you might have more specific ones that you haven't even thought about in years, building a regular mindset practice can help.

> If you want to dive deeper into the subject of limiting beliefs, read *The Big Leap* by Gay Hendricks (HarperOne, 2009) or *Feel the Fear and Do It Anyway* by Susan Jeffers (Vermilion, 2012). You can view a free worksheet of my Top Ten Money and Mindset Books (Handout #2) at www.sixfigurefreelance-book.com/resources.

Here are some examples of mindset work to help you level up into your new earning potential and more confident self:

$ Journaling daily

$ Gratitude reflections

$ Meditation

$ Yoga

$ Positive affirmations

$ Reading/learning/personal development

$ Prayer

As you build a regular mindset practice, focus on being present with your own thoughts so you can address those limiting beliefs head-on. Staying numb to what's happening around you is a coping mechanism that can prevent you from having to dive into those uncomfortable feelings and limiting beliefs. But it also blocks you from your next level of success. Whether it's watching hours of TV, compulsively shopping, feeling like you need to nap throughout the day, scrolling mindlessly through Facebook, or something else, this behavior typically provides little to no benefit aside from helping you avoid confronting your feelings.

If you feel that you're looking for ways to escape often, starting a mindset practice will force you to dive into some of those limiting beliefs or past memories. This process can be painful. You may find that you end up crying or journaling out some internalized feelings and beliefs. Lean into those feelings—this is one of the only ways to process the thoughts that have been holding you back.

## The Beginner's Guide to Building a Mindset Practice

If you're looking for the magic bullet to perfect business mindfulness, you won't find it here. A mindset practice looks different for everyone, and the key to keeping it consistent is finding the practice that really works for you. That said, there are some common themes when it comes to finding what works, which you'll see in some of my suggestions below.

For example, many of these practices require you to step away from technology, get quiet, and sit still. I know that's not easy. Try starting small and working your way up. The longest I could sit still when I started was five minutes, using a guided meditation through my Bluetooth headphones.

Over time, I got better at sitting still or using a walking meditation to think about where I wanted my business to go next. But I still can't sit quietly for longer than 15 minutes. Don't beat yourself up—just do whatever you can and do it consistently.

There's a lot of focus in this book on concrete things like systems and revenue. But those metrics don't capture the full picture. How you feel about your business and how excited you are to work every day are just as valuable, if not more so, even if they are often underestimated.

Check in with yourself regularly (whether that's daily, weekly, monthly, or quarterly) to gauge how you are feeling about your business.

Now that you have a firm direction for where you're headed, it's time to think about not just recognizing your limiting beliefs, but changing them.

### Turning Old Limiting Beliefs into Empowered New Ones

As you work through your mindset questions, begin to tackle the limiting beliefs that could be holding you back. It's not enough to acknowledge them as limiting beliefs (that's just the first step). Your brain has already accepted them as true, so you have to rewire those perceptions into more powerful statements that help you set and achieve big goals for yourself.

Reframing these beliefs is what happens when you do the mindset work. Let's take "There's not enough money for everyone" as an example. To reframe this limiting belief, start by writing all the reasons this statement is not true. Here are some samples:

§ There's plenty of money for everyone.
§ There are many clients out there who would benefit from my services.
§ By making more money, I get to serve more clients with my valuable work. I then get to create more economic opportunities for others as I hire subcontractors.
§ As a freelancer, I get to create my own opportunities.
§ I have access to many projects, clients, and income streams because I live an abundant life.

Writing, reading, or saying these new beliefs out loud can, over time, change your thought patterns. But this is not a "one-and-done" process. It often requires digging deep into where that limiting belief originally came from and working hard to rewrite it. When you uncover a limiting belief, ask yourself if it's really true or if it's something you picked up or accepted as true somewhere along the way.

The example above is a general limiting belief about money and scarcity that can be common for freelancers. There are plenty of other limiting beliefs that crop up again and again in the freelance community.

Below are some examples of how these limiting beliefs can show up in your own inner dialogue, as well as suggestions for how to reframe them.

A lot of them are related to money because the connection between money and mindset is strong, but there are many different ways your mindset can trip you up. The goal is to become more aware of what limiting beliefs look like so you can spot your own.

## I Don't Deserve to Make Money

It might seem crazy, but the idea that you don't deserve to make money pops up a lot with aspiring high-level freelancers. The roots of this can vary. Perhaps your parents work really hard for the life they have and it doesn't seem "fair" that you get to work from your computer, making decent money while working less. Maybe you're concerned that you're not good with money, and therefore you don't deserve to have it in your life.

Thinking that you don't deserve to have money can block you from making it. Don't believe me? There's a type of freelancer who gets off a phone call determined to quote $2,000 for the project they just discussed with the client, but in the end they send off a proposal for $1,200. Their post-call thought pattern goes something like this:

> *I'm going to charge $2,000. It's the right price for this project, based on what I heard. But $2,000 is a lot of money. If I throw this out there, the client might decline the project altogether. I don't want that. Maybe $2,000 is too much. I have only been offering this service for six months, so I'm not really qualified to command a rate like that. Maybe if I drop my price, the client won't be able to pass up the deal I'm offering. What about $1,600? That still seems like a lot of money. The client might laugh in my face even at that number. I mean, there are people out there charging a lot more than that, but I'm not one of them. Who am I to say this costs $1,600 anyway? I don't want to deal with the awkward back and forth if the client says it's too much. Maybe $1,200 is fair. It's probably a little less than what the average person will charge.*

See how this went from a confident pricing position all the way to hoping the client will accept a proposal for $800 less? Freelancers do this to themselves all the time, talking themselves out of what their intuition tells them to do. Those limiting beliefs can pop up anytime, and they often arise around money.

Finding the root of why you think you don't deserve to make money will help you reframe this limiting belief. If you believe, for example, that you don't manage money well, reframe this by saying, "Making more money gives me an opportunity to expand my awareness and practices with money. I look forward to investing it, paying down debt, and using this new income."

### Money Will Ruin My (Insert Relationship Here)

Are you worried about being a primary breadwinner or just nervous about how shifting money dynamics might influence your relationship with your partner? Afraid those relatives you never talk to might come out of the woodwork asking for loans and cash because you're now rolling in dough, at least from their perspective?

Finding out why you feel this way can help you develop a more positive relationship with money that makes you feel more confident about earning it. Here are some examples:

$ "Making more money doesn't mean I have to tell the whole world about it. I'm excited about earning more money because of the opportunities it will afford me and my family."

$ "I have great boundaries with family members and friends. Earning more money will allow me to help people when I choose to."

The great thing about reframing your beliefs is that you get to decide how you'll approach these subjects in the future. Choose a reframing statement you can really get behind. Whenever you notice that limiting belief bubbling back up, think about whether you need to do more reframing work around it. If you feel uncomfortable talking about money in front of your family, perhaps you notice that Thanksgiving dinner each year is a trigger for you, when relatives tend to make comments about how successful (or unsuccessful) they perceive you to be. Use your reframing statements to help yourself cope internally, and think about how you will handle these situations and triggers in person.

### I Have to Work Really Hard to Make Money

This limiting belief addresses the idea that you might not feel as though you're working "hard enough" to earn your money. In other words, if you earn money "too easily," you don't deserve it.

Maybe earlier in your life, you had to work extremely hard, putting in long hours. Or when you launched your freelance business, you were doing so as a side hustle, burning the midnight oil after your day job. What started as a necessity can translate into an ongoing work ethic. Most freelancers who level up their business look back and are shocked to realize that once they mastered mindset, client selection, and scheduling, they were putting in fewer hours and making more money (and likely had dumped the soul-sucking clients they had in their early days, too).

This can be hard to reconcile. Why was it so hard then? Why does my spouse work so hard at their job? Why do most of my colleagues feel pressured to do more to impress other people, as if there's an award for putting in the most hours at your job?

Here are some possible reframes for this limiting belief:

§ "I don't have to work as hard as my parents did to make money, but that's probably what they hoped for me, anyway!"

§ "I get to provide a service I love at a cost that reflects my value, and I leverage technology to get the job done faster and easier. No one should hold that against me!"

§ "My parents worked really hard in this life, but I love that because of that, I get to spend more time with them and help them if I choose, based on my ever-growing income."

The bottom line with these reframes is that you don't need to feel bad about being good at what you do or having a financially successful business. You can build a successful business for your own reasons or help your family if you want, but the root feeling of guilt shouldn't be there.

### Money Will Change Me as a Person

Sara Blakely, founder of Spanx, has a great quote: "I feel like money makes you more of who you already are. If you're nice, you become nicer. Money is fun to make, fun to spend, and fun to give away."

If you're a kind, generous, and wonderful-to-be-around person, why wouldn't you be that same person with more resources? Imagine how your ability to give to a charity you love or help your family could be expanded by a higher earning capacity. It's easy to default to the idea that money makes you "greedy" or "power hungry" or "rude to others." But there are plenty of people at varying income levels who act that way, and there are plenty of people who choose to act the same or even better when they earn more. You decide. Money doesn't have to "change" you for anything but the better.

Here are some ways you can reframe this:

$ "I'm already a good person. There's no reason to think that won't still be the case when I create more economic opportunities for myself and my family."

$ "There are a lot of causes I've always wanted to support in a bigger way. I'm excited to be able to improve my own finances and give back, too."

You don't have to become a monster just because you generate more revenue or take home a higher income for yourself. You get to decide what the future looks like, and it doesn't mean giving up who you are or who you aspire to be.

### If I Make More Money, I Might Start Valuing That as My Key Metric as a Person

Most humans strive to be well-rounded individuals, so it's natural to be afraid that you might start judging yourself by one personality trait or accomplishment. I recognized after a few years of high-level freelancing that if I fell short of my income goals for the month, I beat myself up about it.

There was often more to the story, however. Maybe I fired a terrible client and had less income for one month while I restabilized, but I was happier overall and was finally charging more in line with the value I brought to the table. Or maybe I was just on vacation for a week or sick for a few days and put my health as my top priority. Income might have dropped during that period, but it didn't mean that I had done anything wrong. Not every day is a working day and not every hour is a billable hour, so I don't always look at monthly income alone.

Make sure you track other numbers besides money. Switch your monthly earnings analysis to every other month or quarterly if you find you're basing a lot of your success measurements on revenue and leaving out other metrics, like hours worked or your general happiness.

Here are some ways to reframe these kinds of thoughts:

$ "Yes, one of the ways I measure business growth is through revenue or profit generated. But I also have and will track other metrics that are equally important."

$ "Having a financially strong business is only one aspect of me or my company. I also love the impact that I have on other people and their successes."

You need to decide what to put into place to ground these reframes in reality and make sure you're not just tracking money. If customer service is important to you, maybe you should also look at customer survey results when you're done with a project or conduct regular subcontractor interviews to ask about your leadership style.

### I Deserve to Have Bad Clients

This might be one of those limiting beliefs buried so far down that it hits you randomly after a few weeks of mindset work. If you have a roster of clients you can't stand working with but it turns your stomach to think about firing them, this might be your limiting belief. If you don't think you're good at what you do, if you think it's "too easy" for you to complete your projects, or if you feel guilty because you get your work done in three hours a day, you might be tempted to bring on more bad clients who help you even out what you perceive to be the positive aspects of your business.

Easy reframe: No one *deserves* to have bad clients.

Here are some other ways to reframe this limiting belief:

$ "There's nothing wrong with wanting to work with enjoyable, pleasant people."

$ "I don't have to tolerate difficult personalities in my personal or professional life if I don't want to."

$ "Even if I make a mistake on a project, I can recognize when some-one has crossed the line into harassing or abusive behavior and I know how to remove myself from that situation."

You deserve to work with people who help you bring out the best in your product and working style. Working with clients who drain you doesn't serve you or the client.

### I Don't Want Any More Clients Because My Clients Are Awful

If you have the wrong clients or are feeling completely overwhelmed by an "energy vampire" client who is consuming all your time, you might stop marketing altogether because working with a nightmare client has become the new normal. If you're unhappy with your current clients, why on earth would you want *more*?

This is another one of those beliefs that you might not realize you have until you start to unpack some of your resistance toward marketing and doing more sales calls with potential clients.

Here are some ways to reframe this limiting belief:

$ "I am taking note of when I don't feel motivated to work with someone, and I always lean into figuring out why."

$ "It's perfectly OK to end a business relationship with someone who drains my energy."

Remember, you are the CEO. You get to decide who you work with and how. Claim ownership of that power!

There are many more limiting beliefs out there. You most likely have some that are unique to you; you can only discover them through the important but sometimes difficult task of mindset work.

## Get Started and Embrace the Journey

In my interviews with 19 other six-figure freelancers, one of the ideas that came up again and again was embracing your journey and jumping in feet first. Even if your freelance gig is a side hustle right now, if you have dreams of scaling it to a full-time income, keep that dream in the back of your mind as you build a plan to get there.

Your path will probably look different from other freelancers. It's hard to listen to a story about how one freelancer scaled to six figures in one year when it took you two, but it doesn't mean that your journey is any less meaningful because it took longer or had more obstacles.

There will be times on your path when you don't feel like you're firing on all cylinders, when you feel like you're falling behind your peers, and when you're not sure if it's going to work. But if this work is really your passion, keep tweaking and growing a little bit at a time. As six-figure freelance writer Ana Reisdorf noted, "Stay the course. It might be slower than you expect, but you will get there."

Overthinking and waiting until things are "perfect" is a common mistake for a lot of freelancers. As six-figure writer Seraine Berube noted, "Jump before you're ready. I spent a lot of time reading, taking courses, following the 'experts' in the field, and never taking any action. I was scared I'd screw up. As a perfectionist, nothing scared me more. Once you have the knowledge, you have to apply it. Sometimes you won't feel ready, and that's OK. Start with some smaller projects to see how it goes. If you enjoy it, then expand upon it. You'll always hold yourself back if you wait until you 'know' everything you feel you need to know for success."

Knowing your own personality is key to knowing when you're hesitating unnecessarily and when you really need more time or resource-gathering to go to the next level. I like to use the CliftonStrengths test shared by Becca Syme and developed by Donald Clifton to learn more about my top five strengths and how they can help or hurt in business. Although Becca Syme's books are geared toward writers, all freelancers can benefit from the CliftonStrengths materials and Becca's interpretation of them. Check out her YouTube show *The QuitCast* after you've had a chance to take the CliftonStrengths test yourself.

One common theme that's true for a lot of creatives, regardless of their CliftonStrengths, is the mistaken belief that you need months to learn enough to consider yourself an expert.

Online business manager Melissa Froehlich echoed this concept. She said that it's essential to "Start before you are ready. Don't be afraid to try lots of things. You will never fully feel 'ready' if you don't claim that status that you're going to make a leap."

This theme came up many more times in my interviews. Veteran copywriter Ana Gotter said that it's all about using that initial confidence to build momentum. "It may feel slow to start, but getting your foot in the door can be the hardest part. Getting the rest of you all the way through that door isn't exactly easy, but once you've got a few steady clients and your name starts getting thrown around, the business's scaling can happen much more quickly than you'd think. You just have to be ready."

Don't feel like you have to start working full-time right away in your business to embrace this advice. As freelance financial expert Katelyn Magnuson shared, keeping your day job to build your foundation is a very successful strategy. I stayed in my day job for 13 months while I grew my client list and tested my systems, and Katelyn didn't leave hers early on, either. She said, "Keep your day job longer than you think you should. It gives you time to build up an emergency fund, only take on clients/projects you want to work with, and puts less pressure on your business."

As you can see, a lot of these six-figure freelancers think alike—their common habits and mindsets really help build the kind of business you want, no matter what service you offer. What follows are 11 things that six-figure freelancers tend to have in common that help them scale successfully and build their business around their life.

## Habits of Six-Figure Freelancers

Even with different service offerings, schedules, and client loads, six-figure freelancers tend to think and operate differently from those service business owners who struggle to make ends meet each month. Being aware of these habits in addition to doing the mindset work we discussed earlier can open your eyes to a new way of doing business. Let's take a look at 11 habits of successful freelancers that you can start working on today.

### 1. Make a Regular Mindset Practice

Advanced freelancers don't just try to implement strategy after strategy and hope that it works. They engage in mindset habits that keep them positive, like reading books, listening to uplifting podcasts, journaling, yoga, massage, exercise, and more. Six-figure freelancers know that getting their mindset straight is *almost* as important as the work, and some days it's even more important.

They commit to spending time reading, meditating, journaling, or doing their mindset practice of choice daily or weekly. They continue to identify new limiting beliefs or limiting habits and develop a plan to reframe them.

### 2. Don't Get Attached to the Outcome of Any One Thing

Successful freelancers know that no one proposal, pitch, or phone call defines them. Instead, they approach their opportunity calls with clients with confidence rather than desperation. And that can make a world of difference when you're on the phone with a potential client.

If they make a mistake, these freelancers make a note of how to avoid it in the future and move on, rather than spending days lamenting a failed proposal they thought was a sure thing.

### 3. Avoid Underpricing and Overselling

Savvy freelancers don't promise the sun, the moon, and the stars just to get the client to say yes. Instead, they know their value and they ask for it, even though they know that means many of their potential clients will turn them down. You will always be too expensive for some people. Six-figure freelancers don't try to convince the client that they can "do it all."

Unless you love juggling multiple things at the same time, niching down or focusing on the things that you do best is a great way to build your business sans burnout.

### 4. Avoid Drama Impacting Your Business

Smart freelancers don't engage in unnecessary drama with friends, family, or anyone else, especially online. Do you really need one more space where people are arguing with each other and shaming one another?

Six-figure freelancers are too busy running their companies, delivering client work, and growing their mindset to be worried about naysayers.

## 5. Double Down on What You Do Best

Smart freelancers don't try to offer 50 services in an attempt to appeal to *everyone*. You can still have a lot of interests and possibilities on the table without overwhelming clients and making people wonder if you really can deliver the same quality across all 50 services and packages. Figure out what you like to do, what's in demand, and the right mix for providing variety instead.

## 6. Always Be Marketing

The most successful freelancers I know don't stop marketing even when they're fully booked. Instead, they use that to their advantage. They establish waiting lists. They use urgency and scarcity to convert new clients. They think about which marketing avenues deliver results and don't fall into the trap of trying to use every single marketing option to bring in potential clients.

You'll learn more about marketing in Chapter 5, but for now, know that you must spend time marketing your business every single week to keep your pipeline constantly full. What you do in that marketing time might vary based on your current client workload, but you should always be doing something.

## 7. Position Yourself and Your Time with Value

Six-figure freelancers try to qualify clients before they talk on the phone to avoid the "tire kickers" who just want to ask a lot of questions about strategy but have no intention of hiring you. They recognize when a client is not the right fit and conclude the conversation or sales cycle promptly and professionally. They say "no" to projects that don't light them up, pay too little, or are managed by difficult clients.

These freelancers seek ideal clients only and often have a per-client or monthly minimum. They won't take on a project where the work has a defined scope per month or where the client is paying a flat fee, but that also includes hours and hours of uncompensated phone calls.

### 8. Know When to Ask for Help

These freelancers see opportunities for collaboration, outsourcing, and coaching as ways to leverage their existing success. They recognize that they need support from a variety of different professionals, including an accountant, perhaps a team of freelance subcontractors, a virtual assistant, or even a coach. And they see these professionals as investments rather than an expense, outsourcing what doesn't fit in their zone of genius and keeping the rest. Your *zone of genius* is where you are doing work at a high level that only you can do in your business. It's most likely speaking to prospective/current clients and working in your service area. If you work in graphic design, for example, your zone of genius is probably analyzing existing visual work or creating incredible visual materials. That means a whole lot of other things that have to happen within the business, like answering email, publishing blogs, or keeping work samples updated on the website, don't need to be done by you. Maximize the time you spend in your zone of genius.

### 9. Accept Responsibility for What You Can Control

Six-figure freelancers know that they're in the driver's seat for their business. They accept responsibility for what they do—marketing, speaking to clients, and delivering solid work. They don't make excuses like "My market is oversaturated and I don't intend to adapt as a result" or "Freelancing just isn't what it used to be."

They don't blame problems in their company on someone else. They recognize the role that they played in that process, so they don't pin their difficulties on marketing tools, virtual assistants, or anyone else. Instead, successful freelancers always look to see where they can improve and then create a solid team to help them get better and accomplish even more.

### 10. Surround Yourself with Winners and Other Lifelong Learners

Next-level freelancers know they're the master of their own company, but they're always looking for places to grow and improve. They inspire other people with their example.

You can build your support system by networking with other freelancers and mastermind groups who can be at your side as you navigate and grow your freelance business. Finding other people who get what you do, who encounter the same types of challenges and obstacles, and who can be a sounding board when you have questions and concerns can be instrumental in helping you scale.

Often, friends and family members don't really understand your work as a freelancer or what it takes to run a freelance business. So build that community around you, even if you're a remote worker at home. Building a network of other professional service providers is a great step if you want to thrive and grow with like-minded peers. We have a list of great online communities for freelancers where you can network with your peers and ask questions at www.sixfigurefreelancebook.com/resources.

## 11. Focus on the Future

Successful freelancers use their experience to build their business around their life, and not the other way around. Six-figure freelancers don't just keep adding revenue to their business, especially if it's also adding complexity and making them increasingly unhappy with the process of running a business. They're constantly thinking about how to do things differently and make their business work more effectively for them.

The more you start thinking about where you're going with the next step in your freelance business, the easier it will be to build your confidence and get to that point. From mindset practices to modeling the habits of other freelancers, you can start being more aware of how you show up in your business every single day and how it makes you feel.

Adjusting your mindset is a process you'll have to return to often as your business grows. There's a saying: "New level, new devil." You might notice old limiting beliefs popping up at different stages or entirely new limiting beliefs emerging. Having that regular mindset practice will also help you succeed whether you're a solopreneur or you intend to grow your company to bring on subcontractors as an agency owner.

## —— CHAPTER SUMMARY POINTS ——

$ You likely have some limiting beliefs that you need to acknowledge and reframe before you can scale your business.

$ Plenty of freelancers have similar limiting beliefs that can be adjusted.

$ Successful freelancers with different business models often have very similar practices and strategies about how they operate. You can learn a lot from following and interacting with others who are like-minded.

## *Resources Mentioned in This Chapter*

$ Top Ten Money and Mindset Books, Handout #2

$ Best Online Communities for Freelancers Handout, Handout #14

# agency vs. solo models

I f you're relatively new to freelancing, you have most likely been operating your business as a solo model by default. This simply means that you're doing all the work of finding clients as well as completing the work for them. If you only have one virtual assistant or backup/overflow provider on tap, you're likely still in the solo model. The agency model implies a bigger team and a different branding and marketing push. Each model has pros and cons and you can always decide to switch from one to the other at any time in the future.

In this chapter, you'll learn more about how these two different models work and how you can use your personality and business management style to decide which of them is right for you. Later in Chapters 9 and 10, you'll discover more about how to outsource properly (even if you choose the solo model, in which case you'll be outsourcing things other than client work). For now, focus on the big picture and concentrate on fleshing out other aspects of your business before jumping into outsource mode.

It's important to note here that outsourcing to a virtual assistant or other freelancers is not the same thing as running your company in an agency model. In an agency model, you distribute most or all of the work for clients to subcontractors instead of handling it yourself. Outsourcing to other experts those administrative tasks that consume your time (like bookkeeping or scheduling) is covered in Chapter 9 and can benefit both solo and agency companies.

## How Do I Know Which Model Is Right for Me?

Determining what is right for you always boils down to a personal choice, but there are several personality traits that can indicate which of these models is more appropriate for your business. A hybrid model, in which you outsource some of your client work but still retain ownership over other projects, could also work well for you. The important thing to remember is that you do not yet have to commit to either model, but having this information in the back of your mind as you work through the remainder of this book will be extremely helpful. Let's take a look at some factors that might determine your model.

Some personality traits that make you more likely to succeed as a solo business owner include:

$ You like working on your own.
$ You don't enjoy managing other people.
$ You have a highly specialized niche in which it's hard to find qualified freelancers to help you (e.g., writing medical copy for doctors' websites, where a certain level of technical knowledge is required).
$ You want to keep your team relatively small but have a few high performers working with or for you.

Some of the personality traits that make you more likely to succeed as an agency owner include:

$ You love selling and converting clients, but might lose steam in getting the project completed. You get your "rush" from booking the client but follow-through is your weak spot.

$ You enjoy networking and communicating with others and find working entirely by yourself a bit too isolating.

$ You have solid enough margins where you could pay another free-lancer a decent rate to complete your client work while still being compensated for your part in winning that business and editing/administering the client relationship.

You may also notice signals within your business that indicate when you need to decide whether to switch to an agency model. That said, simply being busy doesn't mean you must switch; I make a good living running my business as a solopreneur and am happy with my work flow. These business signals, however, are the first sign that you're on the road to being overbooked or burning out, so take a step back and decide how to change your business to accommodate the growth.

These signals include:

$ You're overbooked with work or barely making your deadlines.

$ Your workload is heavy and consistent, sometimes forcing you to turn down projects you'd really like to work on.

$ Your availability might change in the near future, such as recovering from surgery or taking maternity/paternity leave.

$ You feel like the business is too reliant on you; if you needed to take a sick day, you feel everything would fall apart.

$ Your clients are asking for more bandwidth or new kinds of related projects that you don't have the skill set for and aren't interested in learning.

$ You like managing a team and have a good working relationship with your virtual assistant and any freelancers you've worked with on past projects.

If this list highlighted that you're close to being fully booked, you'll need to be strategic about how/if you scale your solopreneur business or whether you want to consider looking at an agency model.

## Running a Solo Model Freelance Business

In a solo model, you'll be limited by how much work you personally can take on, even if you do have a backup service provider that you use occasionally. However, if this model is better suited to your personality, you can be strategic about which projects you take on so you can streamline your processes as much as possible. I felt much more comfortable owning client projects so I could guarantee quality and the same process each time. I actually made more money working as a solopreneur, too, because of the increased "unpaid" time I was taking on as a project manager while running my business as an agency.

When operating as a solopreneur, it really helps to narrow down your offerings. For example, if you're a photographer who offers brand photo shoots, senior photos, baby photos, family photos, actor headshots, live-action sports photos, and corporate headshots, you might have trouble blocking out your schedule and keeping enough backdrops and studio materials. If no one is booking the corporate headshots or if the sports photos don't deliver a strong ROI given the added travel time, consider cutting them from your offerings. Narrowing in on two to three things you can deliver successfully and have clear packaging for helps you scale as a solopreneur.

I found my way back to solopreneurship by first trying an agency model (which you'll read more about later in this chapter). For one year of my freelance business, I outsourced nearly all my client work to a team of 12 writers, one editor, and one project manager. My team was working on a variety of projects for many different clients, and it required me to completely rethink how I operated my business. While I previously had all my processes and systems in place in my head, I now had to articulate them in written form to ensure that the subcontractors on my team were aware of my expectations.

I realized that I had a lot to learn about leadership, management, invoicing, and appropriate pricing. At the end of that year, I decided to disband my team of subcontractors and focus on projects where I could work directly with my writing clients. It took me several months to make this difficult decision, but ultimately it was the best choice for my personality and my goals for my freelance business.

Some of the reasons I chose to move from an agency model to a solo one included:

$ I found that not all my subcontractors had the same commitment to quality or deadlines that I did. I wanted to be the judge of quality for my clients and have firm control over the output.

$ My clients could detect subtle differences in quality when I used subcontractors, often commenting that they didn't feel comfortable paying a premium price for lower-quality work. Many of them asked me directly, "Would it be possible for you to be the only writer on this project?"

$ Most writers ignored invoicing deadlines or requirements, creating a lot of headaches and emails to explain why someone's invoice was never received, why it was wrong, and why their payment would be delayed. As a solopreneur, I could make sure all I's were dotted and T's crossed.

$ I hated having to create rules around their work that I felt were obvious, such as not submitting plagiarized work—or, worse yet, having to redo the work myself when someone tried to slip things like this by me. I preferred to be the backstop for quality work.

$ Team members often came and went, initially excited by the prospect of a lot of work but then tiring out, suffering with personal issues, or not being a good fit for the team. I felt like I was constantly in recruitment mode. With solopreneurship, I could end all that.

That was my personal experience with running an agency model, so your mileage may vary. Your personality and preferences will help you decide if it's time to move from solo to agency. You can test it out in small steps, such as hiring one subcontractor for a few projects and seeing if you feel comfortable scaling up.

### Tips for Going from Solo to Agency

While going solo allows you more control over processes and product, you may not have the same concerns about the management side of the business that I did and want to add extra hands to help you scale. Below are some of the advantages of working as an agency owner rather than as a solopreneur:

$ Taking on more projects at once

$ Removing yourself from the "production" process and instead focusing more on sales calls

$ Getting to take on bulk orders and orders outside your own area of expertise

$ Gaining more leadership skills and management ability to determine how projects should get completed

$ Leveraging skills into more content management and project management consulting projects where you can use the lessons you learn to help other companies avoid mistakes

If you're currently running your business as a solo and are thinking of scaling to agency, here are some tips to help you make that transition:

$ Clarify your ideal client avatars so that new service providers can get up to speed immediately.

$ Write up guidelines for project quality, delivery, and deadlines so you have a clear written reference point for how subcontractors can work effectively.

$ Write detailed job descriptions explaining what you are looking for in subcontractors and/or employees.

$ Provide an example of a finished product for a client.

$ Provide a quick "hit list" of problems that will encourage non-ideal applicants to opt out of applying (e.g., "Not a fit for someone who needs long deadlines and lots of hands-on support, or someone who struggles to communicate project status on Asana").

$ Set up your payment and invoice structure well in advance if you're going to work with more than three freelancers or subcontractors at a time.

$ Review your pricing and determine how much of a markup should be added to account for your or your project manager's time on the project.

$ Screen your applicants carefully and use a test job (more on that in Chapter 10).

Moving from solopreneur to agency typically requires a transition period. Don't try to jump into it overnight. Take a step back and look at the big picture to determine what gradual changes you need to make before evolving into an agency.

## Starting an Agency

If you have a few trusted service providers in your network already and want to expand, you already have a great foundation for your new freelance agency. The primary difference here is branding, so as you shift your role from solopreneur to agency owner, think carefully about the positive aspects of agency options listed above and position them in your marketing. For example, if you're going to work with a diverse team of subcontractors, consider how that might influence your website copy and your pitches. You'll want to pull the focus away from you as an individual to what your *team* can accomplish.

In an agency model, you or another salesperson would be responsible for identifying prospects for your company services or managing the leads that come in through some other form of marketing, such as your website. You would speak to these customers over the phone or guide them through an online screening process such as an intake form.

Your intake form style will vary based on the service you provide, but it should generally include the following information:

$ The customer's preferred contact information
$ How you'll receive access to any guidelines or branding instructions, if needed
$ Login details for any websites/tools you'll need access to
$ The client's goals for the project
$ If applicable, client comments on competitors/styles they like and don't like

You would be the primary point of contact for this new customer until they have been onboarded, at which point they would either continue communicating with you as the project manager or would be transferred to another project manager or directly to a subcontractor. When onboarding clients, the goal is to collect all the information you need to carry out your portion of the project. It limits back-and-forth emails by gathering data in one place, like an online Google Form or JotForm or directing the client to add needed materials to Google Drive or Dropbox.

As you can imagine from the variety of options available, it is vital to define your systems and processes well in advance. It can be chaotic to attempt to onboard your first agency client and realize you have not thought about who will be answering their emails, making revisions, or handling other aspects of the client relationship.

Knowing this information upfront is also extremely important for your team of freelancers. They should understand your professional boundaries, such as when they need to come to you to disseminate information and how they should turn work in. If you haven't had the opportunity to review a freelancer's work, you probably don't want them sending it to the client before you have had a chance to fix any mistakes. Small issues like this can really add up or even cost you business, so define your systems before you even begin recruiting candidates. Your process will likely evolve after your agency has some on-the-job experience, but it is essential to build out a framework first. You'll thank yourself for this when you begin to onboard new freelancers down the road because it will cut down on the confusion. I will cover more about the importance of systems in Chapter 8.

When you run an agency model, both the systems you create and the people you hire will be crucial for how your agency is perceived in the marketplace and for your overall happiness as the agency owner. Hiring the right people for the right roles is key, and you'll have to be very upfront with whether you're hiring employees or subcontractors or using a mixture of both.

## Using Subcontractors vs. Employees

In most cases, you do not need to hire full-time employees to perform client work. It's usually a good idea to at least start someone on the contractor track; you don't want to hire someone as an employee only to find out you don't want to work together for the long term.

This legal distinction is important because it determines whether you need to withhold income taxes and pay unemployment taxes, Social

Security, and Medicare taxes on behalf of your workers (and have a system for doing so, such as payroll software). These payments apply to employees, but not independent contractors. Independent contractors must handle their own taxes, through payment of a self-employment tax on their earnings.

In general, independent contractors are workers who are responsible to their employers only for the results of their work, not how it will be done and what will be done. The degree of control exercised by the worker is the most important factor. If a worker has been misclassified as an independent contractor, the employer could be liable for paying employment taxes. This information is important not just if you're an agency owner outsourcing work to other freelancers, but also in the event that a current client of your own is treating you more like an employee but paying you as an independent contractor.

More often than not, when a subcontractor comes on board, they will do so as an independent contractor. You'll want to speak to an HR specialist or CPA about whether it makes sense to instead put your worker on the payroll as an employee.

Be very careful not to cross the line when treating your contractors like employees. For example, if you hire someone as a contractor but mandate that they be available during specific hours using a computer you've provided and you dictate how they complete their work, this borders on an employee/employer relationship. This exposes you to liability and is illegal. Freelancers are increasingly well-versed on this subject and will call you on it; be very clear in your onboarding documents, hiring posts, and training materials about which aspects of this position make it a contractor role. Most agency owners will pay their subcontractors and employees directly from their own accounts rather than having the client pay them directly. After all, the client is likely paying a premium for you, the agency owner, to manage the relationship. This means you'll need to track all earnings for the freelancer and send them a 1099 at the end of each calendar year.

The bottom line is that unless there are strong reasons to pay your new service providers as employees, don't. It's a lot of paperwork, and you'll need to add formal payroll and tax processing to your ever-growing list of management tasks. Of course, consult with your tax professional and business attorney to determine what makes sense for you based on the structure of your business.

Check out the IRS guidelines on the distinctions between contractors and employees, and make sure to revisit your working relationships with your subcontractors once or twice a year. If your working relationship has changed, it might be time to add them as a W-2 employee. Having a professional bookkeeper, HR consultant, and tax preparation expert within your network is also helpful so you can consult them as you add more people to your team.

## Tips for Outsourcing in an Agency Model

Whether or not you ever freelanced as a solopreneur, building your systems and project management strategy is essential for the agency model. Even if you start small with only one subcontractor, this is the perfect opportunity to test out your systems and make sure you have built a firm foundation before you scale further.

From the moment you set up a project, make the subcontractor's role clear. It's common for agency owners/managers to handle the strategic end of projects by capturing details and making recommendations before passing off a specific task to a freelancer, but this is not a hard-and-fast rule.

If a subcontractor will be speaking with your clients on your behalf, for example, brief them in advance on any special notes. Conduct a phone interview with the subcontractor before onboarding them into your agency to make sure they can add the right level of professionalism to your communication.

### Decide Whether or Not You Want to Tell Clients About Your Agency Status

If your subcontractors will be interfacing directly with your clients, it's smart to be upfront with your clients that their work will be handled by another freelancer. At a smaller scale, such as partnering with one other trusted freelancer, you might not need to tell the client outright that you're outsourcing the work. But if your current structure involves a team of people who will all be involved in the client's work, it's wise to acknowledge this upfront.

For clients to feel confident about a team member handling their projects, they have to trust your leadership. On a sales call, for example, you might prepare them for what to expect in the next step, such as saying, "Once I write up this brief and we have a signed contract, you'll be hearing from Catherine, the freelancer assigned to the project. She'll be your main point of contact for turning in work, but I'll still be available to you."

Other agencies choose to outsource the work without much interaction between the freelancer and the client, which can sometimes be problematic. The agency owner or project manager winds up doing a lot of middle-man communication, especially if the instructions weren't clear from the outset. In this case, an agency should collect instructions and guidelines from clients (or develop their own guidelines) and then hire and train freelancers who are able to meet the needs of a diverse client pool.

For example, Sarah Fox is a developmental editor who gives feedback on the content of both fiction and nonfiction books. She's also a writing coach who helps writers plot their books and finish them. She leverages other freelancers by working with a team of copy editors and proofreaders who correct grammatical errors in her client's books. Here's what her team looks like:

$ Four editors on copy-editing projects
$ An account manager who does sales calls, project management, and miscellaneous admin work

Digital marketing specialist Danielle Oloko uses an even bigger team of 14 contractors to keep things running smoothly. Since she also owns a cleaning company and a few online stores, using an agency model helps her accomplish everything on her full plate. Some of these team members handle smaller client tasks and others assume more of a management or leadership role. The more team members you have, the greater your need for an online business manager or project manager to be the go-between for you and the other team members.

One of the benefits of an agency model is that you can structure it any way you see fit. If you're managing many clients at once, a project manager might be a great hire to ensure that everything stays on track. There's no one right way to build your agency, but a few tips can help you create the team that's going to be most effective for your company:

$ Be able to speak clearly about your target clients and their primary needs.

$ Draft guidelines for what you require when taking on work and finishing projects.

$ Decide which parts of the process you want to be involved with apart from sales (if any).

$ Have a strong candidate hiring process, using test jobs to evaluate for personality and communication style in addition to talent (more on that in Chapter 10).

$ Have a great ability to navigate any problems that might arise.

## Handling Agency Markup

Some parts of your strategy might need to change if you shift to an agency model. Since you will be responsible for hiring, training, and managing the people who work under you in this model, you need to raise your solopreneur prices to cover your time and effort as well as your freelancers' work. If you need an editor or project manager through whom each subcontractor's work must flow in a review process, include this in your pricing as well.

Your team structure and other factors will determine your agency markup from a base freelancer price. For example, if the freelancer's base rate is $100 per piece, you'll want to raise this by 15 to 40 percent, depending on your individual company costs. Most clients are aware of this markup and are happy not to have to screen and train freelancers themselves, so the vast majority will not object.

If you have existing clients used to paying solo freelancer rates, consider how you'll break the news to them. Will you include them in your process at your current rate and handle those contracts directly? Will they be reassigned to a more junior member of your team to maintain the same rate? Or will you increase their rate in accordance with your new policies and structure? Make sure you have properly written guidelines for project submission so that there's no loss of quality in their projects—a client paying an agency rate definitely expects high quality.

## Tips for Switching from Agency to Solo Model

There can be a lot of work involved in switching from agency to solo model or solo to agency model, but you can always adjust the way your business is presented. Prepare for a transition period as you either onboard or off-board team members.

If you decide that an agency model isn't for you and you'd like to scale back down to being a one-person show, there's a lot to manage in terms of expectations from your current team members.

One of the hardest aspects of "closing down" your agency is letting your subcontractors know a source of recurring income is coming to an end. Here are some ways to make that transition as smooth as possible:

$ Inform your current service providers of the last date they'll be assigned work and their final date for turning in work and invoices.

$ Evaluate your client roster—are there clients you can work with on your own? Will you need to terminate some relationships due to lack of interest or high volume?

$ Revisit your marketing materials to reposition yourself as a solopreneur.

$ Look closely at the kinds of projects that make the most sense for you—you might have used different criteria when running an agency, and now you should be specific about what you want to work on.

$ Decide whether your pricing structure should change given that your expenses should be lower.

Much like the move from solopreneur to agency model, it's not always an instant transition from agency model to solopreneur. Give yourself a few weeks or months to get your new structures and processes in place.

## Does My Model Make Any Impact on Conversion?

Plenty of clients prefer working with individuals over a full agency team. My clients asked me many times if I "farmed out work" to others, which implies a negative connotation to the agency model. However, there are plenty of other clients who like to know that you have a team of freelancers on board. Likewise, if a client has a high volume of work, it can be to your advantage to promote the agency model, making the client feel like your team has enough experience and bandwidth to handle their project.

Ultimately, your conversion rates will depend on your market and the quality of your work. Your passion and preference can make you speak more confidently and produce a more seamless experience for clients, so choose the business model that works for you rather than trying to guess what might convert better for clients.

Here are a few reasons clients might prefer a solopreneur:

§ Rates can be more reasonable than an agency.

§ A solopreneur might be able to fit in more rush projects than a booked-out agency team.

§ Most solopreneurs are happy to step in for one-time or limited projects, whereas an agency might request a long-term retainer.

§ Some freelancers have highly specialized skills that wouldn't work well in an agency, but bring them plenty of niche clients on their own.

Here are some reasons a client might prefer an agency:

§ An agency provides more opportunities for long-term, high-volume work.

§ It can be hard to find a replacement for an individual freelancer, whereas an agency has a lot of freelancers available to complete work.

§ An agency might provide access to different kinds of freelancers, so that the client doesn't have to manage many individual freelancers on their own.

The decision about whether to operate your business as a solopreneur or as an agency owner is about timing, your personality, and how you see the future of your company. You can always change course if needed.

As you decide what's best for your business, consider a few questions:

§ Am I comfortable with the current structure of my freelance business? If I've been thinking about changing things, do my plans match with what another model could provide?

$ If I'm going to stay as a solopreneur, do I have the right clients and project types to scale that successfully?

$ If I'm going to run an agency, do I have any of the systems and guidelines in place to start thinking about recruiting others?

## ── CHAPTER SUMMARY POINTS ──

$ You get to decide how to run your business; if the model works for you personally, there is no wrong answer.

$ Agency owners often excel at management, leadership, and project process.

$ Solo owners want to own the processes of sales and project completion on their own.

$ You can succeed with either model in terms of converting business if the positioning, pricing, and work quality line up.

### Resources Mentioned in This Chapter

$ Sarah Fox website: https://thebookishfox.com/

$ Danielle Oloko website: www.thestrategychannel.com

# attracting and keeping high-dollar, high-value clients

Securing high-dollar, high-value clients is essential for scaling. It's entirely possible to get close to six figures without these clients. Trying to grow it from that point, however, can feel next to impossible.

To be able to reach out to and connect with your ideal clients, you first have to know yourself. Who are you? What do you offer potential clients? This is known as your unique value proposition (UVP). It informs your marketing copy, your pitch, and how you position yourself to clients on sales calls and beyond.

Whether you're a solopreneur or an agency owner, you have to know what makes you unique. As freelancing gets increasingly crowded, it's not enough to be good at what you do. You have to be good *and* be able to communicate quickly and clearly what you or your team brings to the table.

If you can't pinpoint what you do and who you do it for, you won't stand out to those high-value clients you seek. In this chapter, you'll learn more about how to find your own unique value proposition and reference it throughout your marketing process.

## How to Craft a Great Unique Value Proposition

When connecting with clients, most of them assume that you're good at what you do. This alone isn't enough to market yourself effectively. It doesn't really help the client distinguish you from every other freelancer when you make statements like, "I've been doing this for two years." The bottom line is that clients care just enough about your background to build trust, but not so much that it overwhelms them. Clients care about what you can do for *them*.

Your UVP is *not* your qualifying statement to show the client you belong in the freelance world. It's your differentiating statement that explains what makes you distinct from other service providers.

Here are some common examples of ways you can stand out in an increasingly crowded sea of freelancers:

$ Level of detail/focus
$ Expertise in industry
$ Niche focus in this industry or on this type of project
$ Extra bonuses you roll into the project for free
$ Guarantees or promises
$ Certifications
$ Aspects of your personality that make you easy to work with

Your UVP should be personal so you can attract the clients that best fit your business and style. While you can get inspiration from other freelancers, never copy them.

## Positioning Yourself to Potential Clients

You have an upper hand over newer freelancers because as someone who has already been in the business for some time, you have actual client feedback to present to potential clients. The client has to perceive three things as they speak with you or review your materials:

1. That there's a need for the service you provide
2. That you have enough experience and interest in their business to be the one to provide it
3. That now is the right time for them to outsource it to you

There are a lot of other freelancers out there, and even if you're highly niched or focused on particular clients, you can't afford to ignore the competition. Given no other differentiating points, the client is likely to shop around and partner with someone who is less expensive or more experienced. Don't give them the opportunity—make the case for yourself.

Your passion for the subject matter can go a long way. When you truly care about what you're working on or if you're genuinely interested in the client's business, that can overcome a lot of the other challenges of getting a client to "yes."

For example, if you're pitching clients in the pet industry but don't have a lot of experience in that area, talk about your passion for animals. Mention your volunteer work at an animal shelter.

## Match Yourself to the Client's Needs

How can you find out what your potential clients need? One great way is to ask them. You can also take a look at their website and social media accounts to see what they might be missing. They will often mention it during initial calls, on a job post, or in some other way so you can discover what's most important to your clients.

And how can you determine the biggest challenges they face? A lot of your clients will have very similar ones. In the freelance writing world, for example, clients typically need help because they:

$ don't have the time,
$ don't know enough about content marketing,
$ lack the confidence to do the work on their own,
$ have problems getting traffic, or
$ have trouble getting their ideal customers to engage with them.

---

## Look for More Than Money

No matter how well a client pays you, they still may not be the right fit for your business. A few years ago, I was thrilled when a client contacted me about a project management opportunity. His budget was $5,000 per month, and I'd be working on behalf of a major corporation recognized as a brand leader around the world (mouse ears and castles). It was a dream come true, until it wasn't.

The client was extremely disorganized. Before we even had a signed contract, he'd call me after business hours and want to know why I hadn't replied to his messages or emails. He even called me at 7 P.M. on a Friday while I was on a date with my husband. I could kick myself for it now, but I was so excited by the opportunity that I left the restaurant and talked to the client in the car for nearly an hour. Despite promises that he would get more organized, I received very little information from him over the next two weeks. I was given big projects with no timeline or instructions, so I took shots in the dark to deliver what I thought he wanted. It was very time-consuming and stressful, but I only heard back from him after hours, so I continued to take his calls.

The pay was high, but the downsides of the job made it a poor value for the long run. After one month, I walked away, and I've never regretted it. I suspect that if I'd stayed, I'd have been on call at all hours and ultimately failed thanks to a lack of training and instructions.

---

Pay attention to what your client has to say about their problems, whether it's in an email or over the phone, and work to position yourself as the solution.

## Choose High-Value Clients Over High-Paying Clients

Often, freelancers assume that any client who pays decent money for a project is worth the effort. But I've found that's not the case when you're building a six-figure business. Instead of focusing on what you'd get paid for a project, think about whether the client is of high value to you. Here are some characteristics to look for in a high-value client:

$ Offer you projects they love at great rates

$ Easy to work with

$ Open to working with you in a higher capacity as time goes on

$ Have connections with others in their industry who might be the right fit for your services

$ Are thrilled to help you build your business by providing testimonials and new opportunities

Digital marketing freelancer Danielle Oloko said that being able to identify ideal clients helped her spot the red flags. She said, "When customers and associates show you who they are, believe them the FIRST time to avoid some of your biggest client mistakes." Over time, you'll develop a gut instinct that tells you something is off. Copywriter Ana Gotter said this gut instinct is her superpower, sharing that it's best to "say no to projects that you have that gut feeling about. Some clients will make your life hell for no reason, and it has nothing to do with you being incompetent; it's just not a fit, or they aren't doing their part in communicating clearly what they want. If you're able to walk away from projects that you have a bad feeling about, do so."

> For freelance copywriter Karine Bengualid, the difference between an intermediate and an advanced freelancer is all about client selection. She noted, "The real difference is those who can say no to potential clients/work. No, because it's not a good fit. No, because there are red flags. No, because they (the client) aren't ready for your services (i.e., they need to do other work first)."

See the difference between a high-paying client and a high-value client? A high-paying client could turn out to be a nightmare, consuming all your time while closing off all those doors of opportunity I mentioned above. A high-value client might expose you to new training opportunities to become more confident with a new skill but might not pay you as much as a way of "bartering" to get a lower rate.

### Be Ready to Walk Away

While it's never easy to walk away from high-paying projects, you must shift your focus to high-value clients. I call them high-dollar high-value because you're still getting paid well but avoiding the hassles that come with a client who only offers high pay, not high value.

If I told you that one of the most important things you need to do to build a six-figure business is to fire clients, would you believe it? My willingness to say "no" and step away from projects that were a poor fit has made a big difference not only in my bottom line, but also in how I feel about my work.

Of course, it's not just about letting your current clientele go—some of them might stay even if they don't measure up perfectly. It's also about filling the gaps you created by firing clients with new ideal clients.

I want you to keep this mantra in the back of your mind as you create your UVP and pitch it to prospects: *I will only work with ideal clients.* Building an ideal client avatar and using it to decide who to pitch, who to convert into retainer work, and who to let go from your roster will speed up your ability to make six figures.

As a freelancer, you control two things: your time and energy. You should direct them only to people you love working with. If you expend your time and energy on clients you don't like, it will cause headaches for you, fill up your calendar, and block you from future opportunities. What if your dream client sent you an email tomorrow, but you were already too booked up with a project you hated?

You must be prepared to work *only* with your ideal clients if you want to break through that six-figure barrier. Committing to only working on projects with ideal clients was the single biggest factor in building my six-figure freelance business.

## Finding the Right Mix of Clients in Your Business

There's a trifecta in the freelance world that makes for great payouts and enjoyable days. It looks like this:

*Working only with ideal clients on ideal projects at ideal rates.*

Is it hard to find all three elements in every job opportunity? Yes. But is it possible? Also yes. I find that most freelancers who are frustrated by having hit a ceiling of $2,000 to $5,000 per month are booked up with low-paying clients or are not marketing their business consistently enough. Whether it's through fear of letting their clients go or a sense of loyalty because they have worked with those clients for a long time, they are making a mistake by keeping them on their roster.

The mentality that anyone willing to pay you is worth your time can kill your business. Any experienced freelancer can tell you that the lowest-paying clients are usually the highest-maintenance ones. You might have some clients who only pay you a few hundred dollars per month. But to hit the six-figure level, you'd need dozens of them! That's a clear sign you not only need to reevaluate your ideal client avatar, but also set up new minimum project requirements.

If you have clients with whom you've worked for many years and you've never asked for a rate raise, it's tempting to keep them on board, especially if they pay on time and are easy to work with. But raising your rates in accordance with your training and experience is just part of the process.

Firing clients is very hard. It's really uncomfortable to end a relationship with a paying client. There's a good chance your low-paying clients will even fight back, because regardless of how much grief they give you, they don't want to replace you, or they know it will be hard to find someone else.

But now that I've gotten more comfortable with taking on trial projects to see if it's the right fit for me and letting clients go when the relationship no longer works for me (or them), I often feel like a weight has been lifted from my shoulders afterward. A large part of success, both financially and mentally, has to do with choosing who you work with.

After reading the next section of this chapter, you're going to work through an exercise to identify your ideal client avatar. Your ideal client avatar is a persona to help you identify your typical dream client's background, concerns, and needs Don't neglect it. This is like hitting the dartboard right in the center circle every time, because soon your senses will be so attuned to whether someone is a good fit that you can avoid the vast majority of projects that aren't right for you.

## How to Identify Your Ideal Client Avatar

To start the process of identifying your ideal client, you'll need to reflect on who you're already working with. If you don't have many clients or wouldn't describe your existing clients as perfect fits, you'll need to create an ideal client avatar.

An ideal client avatar is a fictitious person who represents the kind of client you want to work with in your business. How clearly you define this person will have a direct effect on how closely your brand, messaging, and product and service offerings match the needs of your target audience. It will also dictate how well you can attract, qualify, and sell only to those you actually enjoy working with.

Early in my freelance career, I landed a job writing four articles per week for an estate planning lawyer. He initially hired me for one month. Shortly thereafter, he realized that it would be much easier for him to pass this task off to me every single month. This was the birth of my love of retainer projects and the recognition that here was my ideal client.

The reason I was so excited to work for this client long term was about far more than the money. While it was nice to have a set amount coming in every month, I also realized that his personality and work style were an exact match for mine.

I made a list of all the things I liked about our relationship:

$  He paid his invoices on time.
$  He hardly ever asked for revisions.
$  We transitioned to a hands-off approach after he was comfortable working with me, so I was able to work independently and use my experience to determine what he needed.
$  He was open to my suggestions and ideas about how to improve things.
$  He was very pleasant over the phone and email and replied quickly when I had a question or concern.

I began comparing every prospective client to him, as my ideal client avatar. I had an actual person to use as an example, which helped me figure out whether a new prospect was the right fit. If someone didn't measure up because they were rude on the phone or paid their invoices three weeks late, I knew they weren't a good fit. Having one or two ideal client avatars in your mind when talking to your existing and prospective clients will ensure that you stack your freelance calendar only with those clients you love working with.

Sometimes it's easier to work backwards to put together an ideal client avatar. That means thinking about the personality and quality of your current clients. If you're unhappy with your existing workload or there are aspects of particular clients that make you upset regularly, this is a sign you want the opposite in your ideal client avatar. Let me give you some examples.

I have a personal aversion to people who feel the need to micromanage or check in with me often as a freelancer. I'm pretty good about setting realistic deadlines, and responding to unnecessary emails is a pet peeve. So any client who checks in too often is not the right fit for me. Recognizing this helped me think about the opposite personality trait—a client who allowed me to work independently and trusted my judgment. That became a must-have quality in my ideal client.

It's not just about personality traits, either. The type and frequency of projects should also factor into your final determination of an ideal client avatar. My favorite piece of content to write are blog posts, which are 500 to 800 words in length and designed for a business-to-consumer audience. They are also the easiest and fastest for me to write, so it makes sense that I would take on more blogging projects than white papers or case studies, which take longer.

In the same vein, it wouldn't make sense for me to bring on many clients asking for only one or two blog posts per month. I'd have to spend a lot of time and energy gathering information for a very small payout. Working with my clients on retainer who order more blog posts, however, is right within my wheelhouse.

By now you should be starting to see how personality traits, the type of work offered, and the arrangement it's in (such as retainer or one-off projects) can all help you put together the ideal client avatar most suited to you and your business.

Now, when you're in an email exchange or on a phone call with a prospective client, you can begin ticking off in your head whether this client meets your checklist. Here's an example of my own:

§ Client is easy to communicate with/already knows the industry terminology.

§ Client is ordering retainer work of at least $1,000/month.

§ Client trusts me to make decisions and complete work independently.

$ Client is offering work related to topics within my content skill set, specifically personal injury, criminal, estate planning, or family law.

$ Client is offering payment in a timely fashion (30 days or less) in a manner that's convenient for me.

> After you start working with a client, you'll need to regularly revisit the process of verifying that they are an ideal client, because it's easy to slip into old habits or to find that their behavior has changed or played out in a way you didn't expect.

To figure out whether a prospect is an ideal client, ask pointed questions. If clear communication is important to you, ask them how they typically keep in touch and what an average turnaround time for revisions would be. Get your prospect to answer key questions like this, and you'll weed out people who are clearly not the right fit. I've discovered, for example, that anyone who tells me they have already hired and fired three or more other writers is not an ideal client for me, so I'll ask about their past experiences with freelance writers. Freelancers often forget that these initial screening calls are a chance for them to ask questions, too. Use them as your opportunity to spot those red flags before you're knee-deep in a project.

Ideal clients will be different for everyone, but when your client load is stacked only with the right fit, you'll enjoy your work that much more. Use Figure 4–1 to help you realize your ideal client.

---

### Creating an Ideal Client Avatar Exercise

The information below is also on the Ideal Client Avatar Worksheet (Handout #3), which you can find on www.sixfigurefreelancebook.com/resources.

Your ideal client avatar is a fictitious person who represents the kind of client you want to work with. Having this person in the back of your mind can help you determine whether you're attracting the right clients as well as determine messaging that draws in ideal clients.

Consider the following questions when developing a mental picture of the person you want to work with:

---

*Figure 4-1.* CREATING AN IDEAL CLIENT AVATAR EXERCISE

$ What industry does this person work in?_____

_____

$ Does my ideal client fall within a particular age bracket? _____

_____

$ What does this person look like? _____

_____

$ What is this person's day-to-day life like? _____

_____

$ Why does this person need my help? _____

_____

$ What challenges has this person encountered in the past while working with others?

_____

_____

$ What do I envision our communication structure to look like? _____

_____

$ How will I deal with problems if they arise with this client? _____

_____

$ What is the emotional state of my client before they hire me? _____

_____

Your ideal clients might share some of the same working styles and personality traits like paying you well, having an open-minded approach to working with a strategist and relying on that expert's input, paying you on time, and being easy and enjoyable to work with. The good news about ideal client traits is that you get to decide what they are for you.

*Figure 4-1.* CREATING AN IDEAL CLIENT AVATAR EXERCISE, continued

---

*How to Enhance Your Connection to Your Ideal Client Avatar*

$ Give the avatar a name. For example, if you work with designers, the name might be Denise the Designer. _____

_____

$ Find an appropriate cartoon or stock photo image of this person.

$ Write a mission statement as your ideal client avatar about how they came to find you and what they need. _____

_____

_____

_____

_____

$ When speaking with prospective clients, try to determine whether this person falls in line with your ideal client avatar.

$ Recognize that it's OK to have more than one ideal client avatar, but you're much less effective if you believe that "everyone" is your ideal client.

Now that you've completed the worksheet, either by writing down your answers to these questions or filling out the worksheet in PDF form, it's time to figure out who you're working with right now who doesn't fit that avatar.

---

*Figure 4-1.* CREATING AN IDEAL CLIENT AVATAR EXERCISE, continued

## How to Handle Existing Non-Ideal Clients

Making a commitment to a better business is not easy, but repeat after me:

$ No more low-paying gigs.
$ No more projects where the subject matter is not your expertise, but you take it on because it seems easy.
$ No more heavy discounts without good reason, clients who call you day or night, or clients who kick things back for revisions 20 times.

Those people are not your ideal clients, and the sooner you get them off your calendar, the more time you will have to pitch and land gigs with ideal clients.

Going through this chapter and completing the ideal client avatar exercise may have helped you realize that you're working with some clients who are not the right fit.

Now is the time to walk through your current client roster and see if they check off the magic boxes. While not every single client you work with will be a 100 percent match, make sure your current clients bring the most important qualities of your ideal client avatar to the table.

In some cases, there may be financial reasons to keep a client who isn't ideal until you can replace the revenue they provide. In other cases, it makes more sense to terminate the relationship immediately, such as if the client is abusive or the revenue they bring in is low.

Your first question might be, "How do I fire this client?" But if you're having problems with a current client, you don't have to jump to firing them right away. I always believe in giving clients a chance to correct things. All too often, at least part of the blame falls on us freelancers for failing to set proper boundaries with communication or contracts.

Take a step back from the situation to see whether there were things you could have done better. For example, I once had a client who felt it was reasonable to request three rounds of revisions. I had another who would call or text me at all hours for status updates. Neither made me happy. In fact, I started avoiding their projects entirely because I didn't want to deal with them. Once I realized that I had allowed their behavior by failing to establish boundaries, I was in a better position to course-correct.

For the client who wanted three rounds of revisions, I completed that job and took it as a lesson learned. But in future contracts, I clarified that my quote included one round of reasonable revisions; any requests for changes beyond that point would come at a rate of $xx/per hour. This was very helpful in future projects because we were both on the same page from day one and I had a contract to reference if they tried to push the envelope. For the client who texted and emailed at all hours, I set an autoresponder on my email after business hours and got a business-specific cell phone that I turned off at the end of my workday. This helped address the ongoing concern with that client and prepared me for better relationships with clients in the future.

But if you've tried to make things work with an existing client and haven't been able to find a solution, it might be time to let the client go. It's very important to approach this process with the right mindset to not burn any bridges while setting a firm boundary.

If you decide that you want to lose this client but aren't quite ready to end the relationship today, set a deadline. Give yourself a firm timeline to replace the client's revenue. At that point, you will have the freedom to walk away.

For example, if the client brings in $500 per month in recurring revenue, set a goal like this: "I'm giving myself one month to turn up the heat on my marketing efforts so I can replace this client. As soon as I have a new signed three-month contract from someone at this rate or higher, I'll notify my current client that our relationship is wrapping up."

If you don't set a deadline and then follow up with the aligned action (marketing) to make this happen, it's very easy to slip into complacency. Working for a client you don't like or on a project that doesn't light you up isn't serving you or them. The sooner you can exit the relationship, the better off everyone will be.

### How to Know Whether a Client Is Worth Keeping

Not every single person I work with is a 100 percent fit with my ideal client avatar. I make some exceptions:

- $ I will consider working with them if it means adding a new skill set I'm interested in acquiring.
- $ I will consider working with them if I strongly believe in their mission.
- $ I will consider working with them if it gives me access to many more ideal clients.

For example, I accepted a copywriting client six months ago. Copywriting is not typically in my wheelhouse, as I mostly do SEO blog work for lawyers or project managers. However, this client has thousands of my ideal clients—lawyers—in their contact list and has already referred me to several of those contacts. Furthermore, working on this project has dramatically improved my copywriting skills. I now have a new sellable service with strong testimonials and references, and it's been a nice change of pace from my typical SEO work. It's new work, I believe in their mission, and I've already been exposed to more ideal clients just by doing it.

You can adjust your ideal client avatar if you realize you've been too restrictive, relax the rules, or change them if, like my situation above, a job presents itself that you just can't pass up. Just make sure the client meets your other requirements to be an ideal client.

## Review the Contract Before Canceling It

The first thing to do when you're thinking about ending a project is to look at the contract. You may have signed something stating that you need to provide appropriate notice. Beyond meeting your legal obligations, this is a good courtesy. Giving the client one to two weeks of notice will help them find someone to replace you with minimal turnover time, but longer periods like a month may be necessary if you're in the midst of a big project. When you do communicate with the client about ending the contract, you may want to reference the contract terms, such as, "Per our agreement, work will be completed by March 31st and the contract will terminate on that date."

## Remain Firm and Professional

The second thing to keep in mind when ending a contract is that you must be firm. In many cases, difficult clients may have criticized you constantly, but they still don't want to look for another freelancer. They might never admit it to you, but these nightmare clients may even know they are getting a good deal, given your expertise and rates, and be reluctant to lose it.

If you know it's the right thing to do, however, let the client go. They may try to sweeten the pot to get you to stay, but this rarely works out. In fact, every client case in which I tried to end the job and stayed on longer because they sweetened the pot ended anyway. Why? Because despite their wheedling, they didn't change the behaviors that made me want to leave in the first place.

I once had a client with whom I had worked for three years. He was very nice and always paid promptly, but after doing the ideal client exercise, I realized there were a few things about the project that didn't match up with my ideal client avatar. First of all, the project was to write a press release once a month, and the pay was far too low. Furthermore, that one press release took a lot of back and forth: emailing his clients to pick topics, draft it, have it edited, and publish it. That was a large time investment, which broke one of my ideal client rules: "Needs minimal email or communication from me." I had to let the client go. He was surprised, but I made sure to end things professionally by giving him one month's notice and helping him find a replacement.

One way to avoid the problem of a client pushing back when you try to terminate the project is to give them a firm departure date. You don't need to tell them why you made the decision; it's better to keep personal details and emotions out of it.

I like to keep my statements brief, firm, and clear: "Unfortunately, I won't be able to continue on in this contract past April 1. My business model has shifted, and I'm now only available to work with a handful of my longtime clients. I regret I won't have time to work on your project. Here's how I propose we wrap up." If true, instead of saying your business model is shifting, you can give some other reason, such as needing to spend more time on a family issue, accepting a bigger role with an ongoing client, etc. Don't tell the client you hate working with them. It achieves nothing and could make things more difficult as you conclude the existing project. Being the one to end the relationship also makes it clear what you are and aren't willing to do. It puts you in the position of power.

If you have referrals to other freelancers, you can pass them along if the client was easy to work with. But do your fellow freelancers a favor and avoid giving them nightmare clients. If you hated working with this person, don't hand them off to someone else. If it's just that the project was too small or not in your wheelhouse, consider making a referral to someone better suited to it.

You should keep your emotions out of the client-firing process because there's no reason to make anyone upset. You'd be surprised—even clients you've fired may refer people to you in the future or leave you positive feedback on a job site like Upwork or on your LinkedIn profile. Even if the client was violating your contract or otherwise impossible to deal with and pushes back about why you're ending the contract, try to remain neutral. Only get into details about their exact violations if you're in the midst of a legal dispute over money owed to you or the work product. If you are in that situation, avoid ending the contract until you've been properly paid for the work completed.

Firing a client is one of the hardest and yet most important things you'll do in freelancing. I've never regretted firing a client. Instead, I often felt a sense of relief because I could refocus my efforts on my existing ideal clients while leaving a space open in my calendar in case another great one came along.

Now that you know more about who your ideal client is, how many of these clients are already on your roster? How many would you need to add to meet your revenue goals?

## — CHAPTER SUMMARY POINTS —

$ You do not need to work with everyone as a freelancer. Identifying your ideal clients and targeting them with your marketing will help you grow your business with projects and people you enjoy.

$ The more you can recognize red flags with clients early on before you sign a contract, the better. However, it's not always possible to identify these people upfront.

$ When you have to exit a client relationship, remain firm and professional, exercise the language in your contract, and give the client a clear expectation of when and how the relationship will end.

### *Resources Mentioned in This Chapter*

$ Ideal Client Avatar Worksheet, Handout #3

# marketing for the advanced freelancer

Any experienced freelancer knows the importance of sales: If you're not confident in or willing to sell your service and yourself, you'll struggle to make money. The more comfortable you can become with the idea of sales as a way of servicing your clients, the easier it will be.

There are many different ways to market your freelance business, and there is no one tried-and-true solution. The only aspect of marketing that applies to all advanced freelancers is that it should still be part of your process even if you've succeeded on just referrals so far. No freelancer should have only one or two methods of getting business. Having a few "hot" sources of freelance leads and a few backup sources to apply pressure to as needed covers a lot of ground. In this chapter, you'll learn more about how to make marketing work when you're also growing and scaling your business and are solidly booked with client projects.

You might be tempted to breeze over this chapter if you're already fully booked. Beware the false sense of security that provides and read on, because the next section includes four signs your marketing process might not be working for the long term even if it is working *today*.

And if you already know you could do better with marketing (and can't we all?), read on to see if any of these warning signs are blocking you from growth.

## Four Signs Your Marketing Process Is in Danger

Does your current marketing process have any of these warning signs?

1. You get business only through referrals.
2. You tend to market only when you have to or don't market enough.
3. You're not sure what converts best, so you do "all the things."
4. You spend a lot of time marketing with very little results.

Let's walk through each one so you can identify it and change course. Then your marketing efforts can start to pay larger dividends.

### Marketing Danger Sign #1: Your Business Is 100 Percent Based on Referrals

Having a referral-based business means that people love working with you. That's a good thing. Having word-of-mouth and referrals as your sole source of leads, however, is not a good thing. Why? You're missing out on the chance to leverage all that social proof in the form of testimonials and use it to your advantage if and when you need to. Would you rather have a system that works until all of a sudden it doesn't, or a waiting list of high-value clients who are ready to spend money on your services?

If your clients value and respect you, put that to work on your behalf even when you don't need clients.

### Marketing Danger Sign #2: You Only Pitch When You Have To

Do you know the length of your marketing cycle? This means the average amount of time it takes for someone to hear of you for the first time all the way to when they sign a contract. It can run the gamut from a week to more than a year. If your typical marketing cycle is longer than a year, you can't afford to sit back and pitch only when your most recent project is finished. That's a long time to wait for your next paying gig.

Every freelancer should always be marketing to some extent, even if they're fully booked. That concept catches a lot of freelancers off guard. Why would you pitch when you have enough work? To give yourself the best thing you can have in business—options.

I can't tell you how many experienced freelancers I've coached who landed one big client or were fully booked for one month and then stopped marketing. Every one of them saw business dry up, were let go by their biggest client, or had to fire their big client. For most of them, it took at least three weeks to get caught up in the pitching and phone call cycle.

This idea of "marketing too much" because of a fear that at some point you might have more work than you can handle is just silly. In the worst-case scenario, you bring on help, give your clients longer deadlines and turnaround times, or use a waiting list. But failing to market is always a bad idea. All it takes is one disaster to set you back to $0.

Here's why that logic behind "marketing too much" doesn't work:

$ Not every client you pitch will be interested in working with you.

$ Even assuming they are interested, plenty of clients will take weeks or even months to get to the contract stage with you.

$ No client is guaranteed to give you ongoing work, and one-time projects can help pad your revenue during slow times or allow you to test out new services and pricing.

$ It's far easier to turn down a client you pitched than to scramble for more work when you lose your anchor client. Remember: You're not obligated to work with anyone. Either party can decide at any point in the get-to-know-you process that they don't want to work together.

Don't let the fear of "too many clients" keep you from always promoting your services. "Too many clients" is not really a problem. You're still in the driver's seat to decide how you respond to that situation—*if* it happens.

### Marketing Danger Sign #3: You're Trying to Do It All

I had a coaching client once who decided that all in the same week, she'd start marketing through her own blog, LinkedIn, job boards, Pinterest, and cold email. But she'd only ever used cold email before, and this was putting way too much on her plate. I recommended that she immediately dial it back down to something more reasonable, like testing out LinkedIn and going from there.

Remember the Pareto principle: 80 percent of your results will come from 20 percent of your efforts. Find the 20 percent that works for you. If you don't have enough marketing experience yet to know what your 20 percent is, run some tests over a period of weeks, putting in your usual amount of marketing effort on one new platform. If you get no results after a month of solid work, it's time to move on.

Many freelancers want a quick and simple answer to the question 'How many pitches should I send each week?' I often get on coaching calls with freelancer clients who say they don't have enough work and then admit they only pitch one or two jobs or clients a week. This is just not enough. While your number will vary based on your marketing method, a good recommendation to follow is ten pitches per week on job boards like Upwork and five cold email/LinkedIn pitches per week if you want to consistently engage clients and open conversations. Using this as a starting point, you can set some weekly goals to help you accomplish ongoing pitch work. You have to pitch consistently and in high enough numbers to generate conversations, but that doesn't mean holding yourself to six marketing methods and 50 pitches a week.

Look for the marketing methods that give you the best chance at results. For example, if you're a highly specialized anime cartoonist, there probably aren't enough potential clients on Upwork for it to be worth your time. But building connections in anime Facebook groups and on LinkedIn? That gives you more tailored options to find your ideal clients.

### Marketing Danger Sign #4: You're Getting No Results

If you're getting no results from your marketing—and by that I mean you've had only one client in the past three months or you're sending 25 pitches a week that go nowhere—first and most important: stop. Don't keep using a broken system.

This is where you take a step back and ask a freelancer friend to take a look at your pitch or give you an honest opinion on your freelancing website. You can even hire a professional to give you feedback. As a coach, it crushes me when someone comes to me and says, "I've sent 100 pitches this year and only got two small contracts." If I review their material and see that their work samples were bad or their pitch was a total dud, I just wish they'd gotten help sooner.

If something is broken, stop and try to find out what it is. Remove your personal feelings from the equation. This is business, and if something isn't working, you're costing yourself opportunities by staying too committed to your course.

## Marketing Options for Advanced Freelancers

The easy thing about scaling your marketing efforts is that if you've been in business for some time, you already know what works and what doesn't. You can take the shotgun approach rather than the machine gun: Don't spend hours marketing in ten different ways when only a handful of those are likely to get results.

For me, marketing comes down to three primary sources: current clients/referrals, Upwork, and LinkedIn. Each of these platforms requires a different approach, but time after time, they are the source of my new business. Occasionally another job board or a post on Facebook will send business my way, but never in high enough numbers to make those platforms a reliable marketing method. Instead, I scan Facebook groups and job boards a couple of times a week just in case something jumps out, but that takes me probably less than 30 minutes per week.

To start with, consider all your current clients and your favorite projects from the past. How did they come to you? What marketing methods get the most consistent results for you? By becoming an expert at those few sources, you're much more likely to successfully scale your marketing in a way that's already getting you conversions, rather than trying to build another marketing method from the ground up.

In general, the most common freelance marketing methods include:

$ Direct contact (cold calls, in-person pitching, direct mail, cold emails)

$ Social media (LinkedIn, Facebook, Twitter, etc.)

$ Your website (which only works if you have a way to drive traffic and leads to it)

$ Job boards

$ Current/former clients

To recap, you don't need to be actively involved in each of these marketing methods. Rely on one or two key outreach options and keep a few other possibilities in your back pocket if the need arises or you want to test something out.

## Tracking Your Marketing

Do you have a method for monitoring the time you spend marketing and the ROI you see from it? The answer for most intermediate freelancers is "no," because they're so busy that it seems too difficult to add one more thing to keep track of, but it's critical to start tracking numbers if you want to scale.

If you could spend two hours per week on a marketing method that generated 80 percent of your results vs. ten hours a week trying all the marketing methods "just in case" but diluting your primary high-conversion method with 80 percent of results, which option would you take?

Freelancers run their marketing in many different ways. For instance, I've never landed a freelance writing client through Twitter. After four years, I let my account become inactive. But I know a freelancer who gets a handful of leads on $400-per-post tech gigs there every month. For her, that's her 80 percent of results. But I was happy to take one thing off my to-do list that wasn't working for me.

Many of my coaching clients get caught in the cycle of compare and despair after they see a colleague share a "big win" in a Facebook group or after a conference with other freelancers. They decide that if that person is so successful on X platform or with that marketing method, they can just copy their success. But this is like asking another freelancer to give you their winning pitch. Pitches and marketing methods are both so customized that what works for one person usually won't work for you.

This leads to a chicken-and-egg scenario: You can't know whether a marketing method works until you test it, but you don't want to waste time marketing in ways that don't get results.

The solution is to lean heavily on your most reliable marketing methods but allow some wiggle room to try new things. When you try something new, try only one thing at a time, be purposeful, and closely track your results. If this is the month you want to try getting work from Twitter, set a numerical goal for how much outreach and follow-up you'll do there. Use a spreadsheet to track your results. If you make a solid effort over 30 days and get zero traction, consider it a lesson learned and put that shiny object back on the shelf. Then you can move on and try something else.

> Testing and tracking is the only way to see if something works for you. Work smarter, not harder. Don't feel tempted to try everything.

If you already have a successful marketing method or two, now is your chance to optimize them for even greater effectiveness. Even tiny levers can lift a lot of weight, so analyze your current procedures and decide if there's a way to do things even better.

If your current clients are a big source of referrals, for example, look for opportunities to maximize your referral program. Have you been offering clients a simple "thanks" when a referral fee or other gift would be more appropriate? Have you thought about implementing a formal referral rewards program but haven't gotten around to it yet? Now might be the time to put your plan into action.

The marketing that works right now is your lever movers. It's what you need to take your company to the next level with minimal effort. Consistent use and tweaking of your lever movers is much easier than trying to learn and master a whole new marketing method.

Since there is so much differentiation between marketing methods and freelance services, there is no one number you should aspire to in terms of getting clients to convert. You might have to send 50 pitches to secure two high-end clients, for example, whereas if you charge $100 for your logo design service, you might be able to get a gig with just three proposals on Upwork. What matters is to use something like a spreadsheet or Airtable to keep track of your marketing.

## Does Niching Make Sense?

Just as you can run your six-figure freelance business as a solopreneur or as an agency owner, you can decide whether or not you want to niche. There are some major benefits to narrowing down what you do by project type, client type, or both. In this section, you'll learn more about niching so that you can decide to either stick with what you've been doing so far, in or out of a niche, or make some shifts to test out a new strategy.

In the freelance community, you'll find just as many people arguing that you should never niche as you will people proclaiming, "The riches are in the niches." So who's right?

Niching might work for you and it might not. I've broken down the benefits and downsides so you can match your personality and preferred work style with wherever you feel the most synergy.

For freelance accountant and bookkeeper Meagan Hernandez, niching was the fast track to more business. She stated, "Pick a niche as soon as possible and shout it from the rooftops! If you are the one that offers everyone everything, nobody will remember you for specific needs that come up." Shopify store builder Leighton Taylor feels the same: "Pick a niche and start saying 'no' to everything else," he said. "This establishes you as an expert in a field and makes you more referable."

Some of the benefits of niching include:

$ Having to master only the software and trends in one kind of project or industry

$ Clearly and instantly communicating what you do to prospective clients who have never heard of you before

$ More easily optimizing your strategies like intake and project completion

Some of the downsides of niching include:

$ If your area of focus gets oversaturated or uninteresting to you and you haven't had the time to learn new skills, your curve to sell something different might be steeper.

$ You might miss out on getting to work on projects that would show you alternative interests or possible future services to include.

$ You might become hyper-focused in one area and struggle to answer some of the big picture questions some clients might have.

If you decide to niche, consider building a network of other freelancers you can pass work to when it's not the right fit for you. Sometimes a current client will ask if you can complete a new project; it's up to you to roll it in as a one-time project and see if you like it. Having a network of other freelancers makes it simple to tell the client that you don't currently work on that kind of project but might be able to recommend someone who does.

If you have the right referral relationship with your fellow freelancers, they might pass projects your way, too! This supports the freelance economy and opens new channels for work to be funneled your way. Make sure you know the exact kinds of projects the other freelancers are interested in working on and discuss whether they might be interested in teaming up on projects, too.

## Niching by Project Type

Rather than working on all the projects in your service area, you can focus on just a few. Here are some examples of what it looks like to niche by project type:

$ A graphic designer who only does logos and branding design boards
$ A copywriter who works specifically on white papers
$ An editor who gives feedback on full-length manuscripts
$ A developer who specializes in Ruby on Rails

Niching down by project alone can provide enough variety to allow you to become really skilled in one particular area. Being known as the "go-to" person across multiple industries also helps ensure branding that is broad enough to bring in consistent client flow.

## Niching by Client Type

Narrowing in on one industry or particular group of people makes it easy to understand their pain points. Here are some examples of freelancers who niche by client type:

$ A health-care strategist who works exclusively with nonprofits in public health

$ A sales copywriter who writes landing pages for business coaches and course creators

$ A virtual assistant who supports only fiction authors

$ A web developer who builds for startups alone

Don't assume that niching means you automatically turn down all projects outside your narrow scope. You still decide when you want to step outside your project/client type comfort zone, so you can always try something new.

### Niching by Project and Client Type

Narrowing down even further, niching by project and client type is a perfect fit when there's plenty of demand for that project within your chosen industry without boring you. If you need variety in your work and the chance to expand beyond certain types of projects, I don't recommend this route. That said, I managed my freelance business for five years almost exclusively writing blog posts and web content for lawyers.

The beauty of niching by project and client type is that you can always branch out and learn something new. I ultimately incorporated email newsletters and public relations services for my clients when I grew tired of writing blog posts. I only took on one or two outside projects like that at a time, but it gave me enough variety that I never felt I was growing stagnant.

### Not Niching at All

If you take on every kind of project that comes your way because it piques your interest, it will certainly provide plenty of opportunities to work on something different every day. This route can be draining, however, as you try to get up to speed with the trends and jargon of various industries. I found it was too hard for me to track trends in website copy, blogs, ebooks, email newsletters, and sales copy, and I couldn't claim expertise in more than one or two of those areas.

## Ten Advanced Freelancer Marketing Tips

What follows are ten tips and trends I've found across freelancers making $5,000 or more per month. Read on below to learn more about some of the most effective methods for taking your marketing to the next level based on the experiences of the 19 advanced freelancers I interviewed.

### Tip #1: Know Thy Client

When you're working on your client's projects, you often put yourself in their customers' shoes. When you're marketing to and speaking with prospective clients, you must constantly put yourself in their shoes.

If you completed the ideal client avatar exercise from Chapter 4, you should already know a lot about your client: their pain points, their obstacles in tackling this project in the past, their overall knowledge about marketing, and more.

From the moment you send out a blog post all the way through your sales call and beyond, this information should stay top of mind.

### Tip #2: Deliver an Incredible Client Experience

Marketing and outreach is the first time a potential client interacts with you, and it should be an indication of how they'll be treated as your clients. Make sure it's a perfect Goldilocks-style balance of showing that you're interested in working with them, but you're not going to have your boundaries stomped.

Here's the win: You can still deliver a great client experience while maintaining solid boundaries with them.

When you focus on making life easier for the client and providing clarity from the get-go, it's easy for them to feel good not just about the quality of your work but about the ease of your process, too. This sets you up perfectly for repeat business.

### Tip #3: Use Psychology to Reflect a Positive Experience in the Marketing and Sales Process

There are many subtle ways to indicate that working with you will make the client's life better. Paint the picture that you're already working together as early as possible. This gets the client in the mindset of envisioning all the ways you will kickstart or improve their business.

Here are some examples of statements you can use to signal this relationship to potential clients:

$ One of the first things I'd tackle if we worked together is . . .

$ That won't be a problem. I've got a lot of tips and strategies to accomplish (insert concern/obstacle the client just mentioned).

$ Oh, you remind me of my other client. Here's a small sample of what we did there and why it worked.

$ I can understand being frustrated with that. It's one of my top goals to make sure that we cross all the t's and dot all the i's.

$ Don't worry, this kind of project doesn't scare me at all. I actually thrive on sorting out all the strategy.

$ If we work together, our next step would be to do X. What I'd need from you is A,B, and C and a kickoff call. It's really that simple. I can take it from there!

This doesn't mean you've committed to work for the client. It just suggests to them that you know what you're doing and that the client is making a huge mistake by leaving all your value on the table if they walk.

When you deliver a great client experience early in the phone call and follow that up by painting a picture of how easy, successful, and even fun it will be to work with you, your client will start to realize that they could offload their project sooner rather than later and focus on getting results.

## Tip #4: Lean In with Current Clients First

The easiest source of business for your freelance company is past clients. These people already know, like, and trust you and are much more likely to consider hiring you for ongoing work or a one-time project.

Keep a relationship with your current clients. Inform them of other services you provide that they might not know about. Reach out organically when you come across a news article featuring them or an interesting study that made you think about them.

If you ever find yourself not having enough work on your plate, turn to your current and former clients first:

$ If you're working on a small project for someone right now, is there a chance to expand that, take on a bigger workload, or put them on retainer?

$ If you sent a proposal to a client a few months ago but never heard back, can you circle back and see if they still have a need?

$ If you last completed a project for a client six months ago, can you check in and see if they have any urgent or upcoming projects you can help with?

Your clients are also a great source of referral business, which is a very common marketing method among six-figure freelancers like Ana Gotter. She advised, "Ask for referrals from your existing clients. They almost always know someone who knows someone who needs someone like you, and happy clients provide the best testimonials. I offer 10 percent off the next invoice if my clients either a) leave me a review on LinkedIn (I always ask that it's honest, positive or negative) or b) refer me to someone who hires me for at least one project. The latter is particularly useful if I'm ever slow, but I haven't had to use it in years."

A marketing blitz to your current and former clients is much more likely to bring in work quickly when you're in a bind, and it's always worth the effort.

There are some scripts on the resources page on the website about follow-up and ideas for connecting with your current clients on a schedule that feels natural. You can find those in Handout #16, Sample Client Follow-Up Schedule.

Your current clients are also the best source of marketing material you can use in your own business when talking to other ideal clients. What are their pain points? What have they loved about working with you? What outcome were they able to achieve because they outsourced to you?

Turn past client words into marketing material and fodder to attract your future ideal clients and discourage non-ideal clients from contacting you through qualifying statements. These qualifying statements can be included on your LinkedIn profile, your discovery call booking page, and the services page of your website.

Imagine that you're an online business manager who plans launches of online courses for clients. Your past clients have all been successful business coaches who were visionaries with very limited time, and who often dropped the ball on details. They often remark how grateful they are that you mapped out the entire launch and left them to do the heavy lifting with sales.

Here's how that experience could be turned into qualifying statements:

$  Are you a business coach who gets great results for your clients and is finally ready to bring that into an online course?

$  Do you want to launch but are overwhelmed by all the work that goes into a 60-day launch plan?

$  Are you looking for someone who can take your excellent sales-closing skills and match them up with the ideal timeline for each piece of the launch puzzle without you having to worry about the tiny details?

$  My clients often exceed their sales goals while avoiding the tech headaches when they hand over the project to me on day one. Sit back, run your webinar, turn on your Facebook ad, and let the sales roll in. It's what I do best.

In those qualifying statements, the experience the client has and the pain points they bring to the table are turned into an experience where the client already starts to imagine what it's like working with this online business manager. The right client will request a call; the person who has unrealistic expectations or who wants some other service, like having the course built for them, will avoid wasting the OBM's time.

## Tip #5: Never Stop Marketing

If you're now comfortable with the 80/20 rule, you might find that some active forms of marketing, like sales calls or sending cold email pitches, are very successful for growing your business. But you might also have access to some low-maintenance marketing methods that, with very little effort, bring in some leads or results, too.

Advanced freelance writer Nicole Rollender learned the importance of consistent marketing the hard way. She said her best advice to aspiring six-figure freelancers is, "Always be marketing and selling. In the first six months of my business, when I felt that I was 'full up' with retainers and work, I stopped pitching and selling. Hard lesson to learn: Two of my retainers, totaling $7,500 a month, ended—the $2,500 one coming to the natural project end, the $5,000 one abruptly ending because the client decided to shutter his doors.

"It took more than two months to replace that income. Now I have mechanisms in place on a rolling basis to keep warm leads in the pipeline, including cold-email pitching, pitching via LinkedIn, reaching out to past clients and prospects, and getting on calls once or twice a week with new leads. That way, I'm prepared in case I need to quickly replace income, and I'm also scaling my business at the same time."

My low-maintenance marketing mode is spending 20 minutes a day on Upwork (connecting professionals and agencies to businesses selling specialized talent) looking for new freelance job leads, a few minutes reviewing my morning newsletters for freelance writing gigs, and taking the time to write one 500-word article per week that I post on LinkedIn and my website.

Sometimes the results are sporadic or perhaps only garner a few leads a month. But given the small time investment, they're well worth the effort. In a best-case scenario, your low-maintenance marketing efforts build on themselves, too. I might get slightly better results if I posted an article twice a week, but that would cut into the time I have set aside for more important activities. And if I only get one extra lead per month from that, it's just not worth doubling my effort. However, posting once a week slowly builds my SEO traction on Google, so over time, that low-maintenance marketing brings me more and more leads every month.

Your low-maintenance marketing might look like:

- $ Connecting with 25 new people on LinkedIn every week (pro tip: copy/paste your connection message into your phone's notes and send these requests out while in line at the grocery store or waiting for your kids to get home from school)
- $ Sending out a custom pitch to three new companies every week

$ Following up with people you meet at networking events

$ Sending two emails a week to past clients to present them with a special offer

$ Pitching two podcast shows a week to come on as a guest expert and talk about your freelance offering and your story

With low-maintenance marketing, you're looking to move the needle just enough to get results, but not so much that it becomes a part-time job. Remember that the goal of scaling a freelance business is to make things more streamlined and process-based. You shouldn't be spending six hours a day pitching your company for new business as an intermediate freelancer.

Low-maintenance marketing should take you at most a few hours per week—even less if you do the work in batches. I found it was easiest to write my four monthly blog posts all in one day and then outsource them to my content manager for editing and publication on a weekly basis.

Don't forget to update your work samples, testimonials, and rates every six months or so. This is also a good opportunity to ensure your pitch is still relevant. If you just completed a big project or got a new certification, for example, a short plug about that might fit into your pitch.

## Tip #6: Use Social Proof

As time goes on, clients will say great things about you (at least they should if you know what you're talking about and you're doing a killer job for them).

Use this social proof to your advantage both personally and professionally. When a client says nice things, it's a prime time to ask for a testimonial. If they're not comfortable sharing publicly, copy and paste or type what they said into your personal "evidence list." An evidence list is a mindset tool you can use to get yourself out of a funk. As you add more successes and positive social proof over time, you can break through your inner doubts by opening your evidence list and seeing all the great things people have had to say about you.

This social proof also belongs in places like your LinkedIn description and your website. I made a PDF of screenshots with all my best client feedback from Upwork and share it with non-Upwork clients, too. If people are saying good things about you, be proud to share it!

Social proof on your website can take the form of a PDF document with all your best client feedback, a testimonials section, or even a blog post with a mini-case study about the results you achieved for a client.

Your website is a great tool for passive marketing. Too many freelancers emphasize their website before they have the experience, following, social proof, work samples, and content marketing skills to really make it work. But when you're an advanced freelancer, it's time to consider using your website to the best of your ability.

## Tip #7: Marketing for Your Website

At some point, it makes sense to set up a website for your freelance business, but only if you have a way to drive traffic there. I did not use a website for three years. Too many people believe that if you launch a website, you'll get leads immediately. After using my website and my LinkedIn profile in connection for a few years, I have some tips for getting the most out of your freelancer website:

- $ *Keep it updated.* Use content marketing to add new material like blogs targeting your ideal keywords. (If you're stumped on how to use SEO for your blog, there are many great tools out there. I can recommend "Stupid Simple SEO" by Mike Pearson as one course that helped me.)
- $ *Post regularly.* Don't set up a schedule to write content five days a week if you don't know you can keep up with that. Once a week is a great guideline; it will take time to build your results, but blogging is a long-term game.
- $ *Make sure you have a professional-looking photo and logo*, if needed.
- $ *Highlight comments from past clients* where you can and share them on social media.
- $ *Include recent work samples* that are relevant to what you're pitching.
- $ *Share your content on social media*, like LinkedIn. (There's some real strategy behind LinkedIn as a marketing method that is explored in more detail in my course, "LinkedIn for Freelancers.")

$ *Install Google Analytics* so you can track your results and website traffic.
$ *Consider other forms of marketing* that can send traffic to your website, like ads and guest posting.
$ *Provide options for clients* to learn more about you with an email marketing newsletter list and opt in.

Once your website is built, make sure you have a plan to drive traffic to it, which is where content marketing comes in. Content marketing is so important in today's online environment because it establishes thought leaders and helps your website rank higher in search results on sites like Google. Content marketing comes down to three things: properly optimized static pages on your website (like service pages and other dropdowns that don't change often), updated blog-style content, and a consistent voice across those pieces of content.

More than 2 billion blog posts are added to the internet every year. That means anything you create for your business, like "about" pages, press releases, blogs, static website content, brochures, and other marketing collateral, has to stand out from the crowd. This is why content marketing calls upon successful people to position themselves as thought leaders with their unique spin on hot topics.

Content marketing also helps to build your brand by establishing brand knowledge and awareness. Think about the company blogs or podcasts you follow. You probably have several specific brands in mind, and you wait until they release new material to follow and learn from it.

Additionally, content marketing engages readers. It's not enough to capture somebody's attention for a short period of time. You want them to come back to your website or other marketing material again and again: asking questions, making them think about things, and encouraging them to interact with your brand.

And finally, of course, content marketing has incredible benefits for marketability and sales. It takes a long time to leverage content marketing, but it can pay off in spades. For more advice on how to structure and use content marketing for your own business, check out Bob Bly's *The Content Marketing Handbook*.

## Tip #8: Invest Time in Updating and Learning LinkedIn

LinkedIn is hands down my favorite way to find freelance business. Known as the social media platform where business professionals network, this site is so much more than a living resume. I spent two years perfecting my LinkedIn strategy to leverage incoming leads and to position myself as a thought leader.

> Need more LinkedIn advice? Check out the resources page on the website for a free cheat sheet on using LinkedIn—it's Handout #4.

You can market yourself on LinkedIn through three different components:

1. Having a great profile that clearly communicates what you do and who you serve
2. Publishing content in your industry or creative space
3. Connecting only with prospects rather than peers by sending personalized connection notes and messages to thought leaders and influencers

If you're curious about whether investing in LinkedIn is worth your time, consider this advice from advanced freelancer and project manager Alexis Gilbert. For her, building organic relationships on that platform expanded her network and opportunities. She said, "I actually met all of my clients through networking on LinkedIn. If you are interested in a company, friend people on LinkedIn and ask to speak to them about the environment. Also, wherever you live, reach out to every staffing firm in the area. The key is to have a recruiter connection in every staffing firm, as they know the best contracting and freelance opportunities as well."

For more information on using LinkedIn successfully to find clients, check out my online course on the subject, "LinkedIn for Freelancers."

## Tip #9: Power Up Your Cold Email Marketing

Don't rely on Facebook groups or Upwork as your only marketing technique. You can get far better results with a customized outreach approach to companies you admire and whose products or services you use.

Cold email marketing refers to writing a pitch to the CEO or CMO of a company you like with a very personalized message in an effort to pique their interest and get them on the phone. Cold email can be a slower method of growing your company, since your pitch has to be perfect, your follow-up has to be spot on, and it can take weeks or months to get that client ready to say yes, but it's worth reaching out to at least a few new people every week through cold emails.

### Tip #10: Track Your Results

Use a spreadsheet to track your results so you can make sure your best marketing channels continue to be the best. You can also use this to spot where people tend to drop off in your marketing or sales process so you can focus on improving that one area, rather than throwing out your entire approach when some of it might have been working just fine.

Numbers don't lie, so tracking when you sent pitches, when you sent follow-ups, if you got to the proposal stage, and what your results were will help you stay consistent with marketing and ensure no one slips through the cracks in the follow-up stage.

If you need some new ideas for marketing, check out Handout #5 on the resources page on the website, 20 Ways to Market Your Freelance Work.

## —— CHAPTER SUMMARY POINTS ——

$ Delivering a great client experience starts in the marketing stage by establishing value and painting an irresistible picture of what it looks like to work with you.

$ You can niche or not—the only thing that has to change is your overall marketing message and the kind of clients you reach out to.

$ Your website is a great tool for marketing, but only if there's traffic coming to it. Investing in content marketing can help you get there.

### Resources Mentioned in This Chapter

$ LinkedIn Cheat Sheet, Handout #4

$ 20 Ways to Market Your Freelance Work, Handout #5

# advanced proposals, packages, and retainers

W hen you first started freelancing, it was probably exciting to work on most projects, even if they were small or you weren't thrilled by the clients. You were getting clients, after all, which meant money and hopefully relationships that would bring you more work. However, one-and-done jobs also meant that you always had to be in sales mode.

But the more you can focus on high-converting packages and retainers, the better your chances will be of scaling to the six-figure point. The better you get at predicting your clients' concerns and leading them along the sales process, the easier it will be to convert them not just to one-time packages, but to retainers, too. A lot of the sales process is complete by the time you write the proposal. If you did your job in the initial pitch and the phone call, the proposal (in which you lay out the details, scope, and cost of the project) is the easy next step toward sealing the deal.

How you structure your service options and pricing impacts every aspect of how you work with clients.

In this chapter, we dive into two key concepts: proposals/packages and retainers, each of which might be ways for you to level up your packaging. It's important to note that retainers are a form of packages and are just a way for you to do more work for the same client, based on the packages and proposals you create. The bulk of this chapter dives into the psychology and strategy behind creating packages that close the deal.

## Writing Winning Proposals

Effective proposals for clients include a few common elements:

$ A reiteration of the client's basic needs, gleaned from either their job post, their emails, or your conversations with them

$ An explanation of the process that subtly mentions the pain points you've collected from them

$ A few options so they can decide which level of service is the right fit for their business right now

Let's walk through these three elements and identify some best practices for creating proposals that will get you the long-term, high-value clients you need to scale up to that six-figure status.

### Address the Client's Needs

To make sure you adequately target the client's pain points, start by listening to them. Leading questions help give you information about what you should include and what isn't vital, based on this particular client's pain points. As accountant Meagan Hernandez said, listening is critical to capturing these pain points. She said, "When you put yourself out there and meet new people, don't just sell, sell, sell. It's important to listen to what people need and want, including the language they use. This helps you craft your services based on what people really need and develop your sales pitch to speak to their pain points." That concept of listening also came up organically with behavioral marketing and automation specialist Jason Resnick, who said, "Don't be afraid of the phone: The absolutely must-do is get on the phone and listen to your existing customers to understand how they talk about you, the value you bring to their business, and for opportunities to help them even more."

You should never feel pressured to create a proposal or package when you don't have the information you need to make a strategic recommendation: It's like trying to answer one of those math questions where you haven't been given all the variables. At best, you'll take a shot in the dark that makes it all too easy for the client to turn down your offer. Keep pushing until you get the information you need.

Which leading questions you ask will depend on the kind of service you offer, but you should definitely address concerns like project length, how often you'll need to check in with the client, and whether you should add any bells and whistles to your standard flat rate for the service.

## Lay Out the Process

Next, provide an overview of your process so the client can see that you are providing them with actionable solutions to their needs. You can do this by providing a scope of work, which is a breakdown of your offerings and process. A scope of work is sometimes used in lieu of a contract, or it can be the first document the client looks over before signing a contract. This document captures all the information from your call in regard to the client's basic needs and your communication with the client and lays it out in terms of deliverables, deadlines, and any information you still need from the client. A scope of work is key before a big project when the client might not be ready to sign a contract but needs to review your offerings or compare you with other providers.

It's important to craft a package or proposal specifically targeted to the client's needs, so they don't feel like they're being presented with generic options. For example, rather than simply proposing four blog posts per month to a client or offering two custom PDFs for lead magnets each month, explain why you're recommending these specific options and how this strategy will be effective for the client and their customers. This could include statements like:

$ I'm recommending four blog posts per month to you because consistent, high-quality content is not just what Google loves for search engine rankings—it's also what keeps your readers engaged and building trust in you.

$ These lead magnets will present a visually appealing and simple design that attracts opt-ins and entices downloads, making your customers more excited about the amazing free content you give them.

The scope of work/proposal is the formal document where you and the client agree on your deliverables, but it's also a chance to highlight *how* you'll do that work. When giving an overview of your process, emphasize how easy it will be for the client. Show them how simple it will be on their end once you're managing the content creation process for them. Even if there are really 500 steps to the finish line, reduce that to a much smaller list of deliverables and action steps for the purposes of closing the sale. No one wants to read a 50-page proposal. Here are some examples of what your process overview might look like:

$ As your virtual assistant, we'll kick off with a 30-minute strategy call to define our plan for the next month and verify I have access to the tools I need. Based on our discussion, your deliverables will be sent to you weekly on Fridays so that you have time to review them the following week.

$ As your freelance software developer, we'll use our five stages of software development to create an eight-month road map from user testing to final review to the product launch day. We'll use weekly check-in calls, a project management board with notes and opportunity for progress review, and monthly sprints to ensure we're all on the same page.

Briefly breaking down your process during the proposal stage makes the client feel relieved that they don't have to handle these details, that you know what you're doing and have clearly done it before, and that they now know what to expect. By now you've noticed that you should be pivoting away from ambiguity and toward clarity with clients whenever possible to help them feel confident about working with you over the long run.

## *Provide Options That Empower the Client to Choose*

If your initial pitch call did not result in the client deciding on a clear number of set deliverables, they are relying on you to make a recommendation in your proposal. You already know that clients who are presented with too many or too confusing options won't choose at all, but clients who are presented with two or three winning packages feel like they're in the driver's seat.

Make sure you're happy with all the package options you give them. If you feel that the scope of work is too small or outside what you'd like to be offering at this stage of your business, send them a simple message letting them know, and refer them to another freelancer if possible. Close by letting them know that if they'd like to explore more options, you're available to make recommendations. This firmly and professionally closes the loop and tells them what the requirements would be for you to work on a project for them in the future.

To help empower the client in their decision-making process, provide a clear distinction between the service packages you are offering them. Include a natural progression that matches the increased service and the higher rate you are proposing.

For example, if your rate jumps from $500 at the lowest level to $1,500 in the next package, read your second package again out loud to make sure it includes a natural progression that justifies the rate increase. Consider the following example packages from a Pinterest strategist:

$ *Package One*: I will create eight pinnable images each month for your blog or podcast episodes and send them to you in a zip file. These will be created with your branding in mind. $175

$ *Package Two*: I will create eight pinnable images, add them to your Pinterest boards with proper links and hashtags each month, and pin them on up to ten group boards per month. $275

$ *Package Three*: I will create up to 12 pinnable images each month, add them to your Pinterest boards with proper links and hashtags each month, and pin them on up to ten group boards per month. In addition, I'll create a link of up to four group boards I recommend you join each month, join them for you, and pin the images there. I'll also provide a monthly report of our growth on Pinterest. $400

Consider calling your highest offering the VIP package. VIP clients get special upgrades and treatment, like responses within 24 business hours or more calls. A VIP discount for your biggest package or premium offering also makes that client feel special. It's amazing how many clients are excited by being recognized in this way.

Within packages, you can keep things as simple as possible. For example, you can say you'll deliver one 500-word blog post to the client by the 15th of the month. However, this limits your income opportunity and potential to provide the client with more services every month.

Upsells should clearly add value for the client while not adding a tremendous amount of work for you. If you're a blog writer, great upsells include adding stock photos, offering to post the blog itself, or writing related blurbs for social media. For a designer, it can include multiple versions of the logo, a branded social media graphic, or uploading the new graphic onto the website.

Small upsells and bonuses work extremely well to help the client perceive they are getting something for "free" for signing a bigger or longer contract. If a client is wavering between signing a four-month or six-month contract, consider what you could include as a free bonus to tip them in the right direction. It isn't really free work in the end, since the client is saving you some marketing efforts and giving you a longer projection for cash flow.

## Packages Make Sense for You and the Client

Packages are perfect from both a psychological and a business standpoint when you've considered the client's needs and the best options for them based on your experience. Let's dive into these a bit more.

### Packages Decrease Ambiguity

If you're too vague in your proposal, clients often default to taking no action at all. If there's any ambiguity in the process, they start to worry that they'll end up paying way too much for things they don't need. If a question crops up about something in your proposal, address it as early in the sales process as possible. For example, will you roll phone calls into your overall price? By pricing out this information early on, you make it easier for the client to feel confident about signing a contract, because they know exactly what they're getting.

Clients hate ambiguity, uncertainty, and the unknown, so they are not likely to outsource anything to you without knowing what it's going to cost and how the project will unfold. Strive to make it seem like you've done all the legwork and all they have to do is sign and pay.

Packages clear up issues around instructions, too. Perhaps your intake call started with a very vague premise statement from the client, like "I don't know what I want." This is your chance to position yourself as an expert and make custom recommendations for their situation.

## Packages Set Expectations

Packages help break down the full scope of the project and clarify exactly what you will and won't be doing on it. Whether you're working on a fixed-price project or a retainer, this is a great chance to set expectations for the client. If you listed that your package includes a one-hour monthly phone call, the client knows upfront that they need to pay separately for phone calls apart from that.

Imagine that you're a web designer, and instead of a full package proposal, you just write up a quick summary of your promise to build a WordPress site for a client. They might assume that's an all-inclusive project and you'll automatically provide a month of free support and maintenance after the site launches, a free designed header on the site, and regular plug-in updates. If there is confusion about something in the package, you can fix it before you get to the contract stage, but this way you have not one but two written documents explaining what is and isn't included in your service.

## Packages Explain What the Client Is Responsible For, Too

Within a package, it's crystal clear what the client has to do so you can both get started and succeed on the project. For example, you can't redesign somebody's website until you have their login information, and you shouldn't have a deadline listed on your contract until it's clear that you need that login to begin.

Your package clarifies what the client needs to do to work with you and what instructions you still need from them vs. what instructions you already have. It evens the playing field because there is much less of a chance that the client will come back in two weeks and say, "Hey, I know you did *this*, but I really wanted *that*." When you present the package upfront and include it in the terms of the contract, it's much less likely there will be any confusion or requests for you to do things outside your scope.

### Packages Help You Plan Revenue

Without packages, it's hard to tell when and how you'll get paid, creating a cash-flow problem. If you don't have enough package projects in the pipeline, it can feel stressful each month to "start all over" with generating revenue.

When you have a monthly revenue goal in mind, like $5,000 or $10,000, you might need to sell a few set packages each month to hit that goal. While $5,000 might seem overwhelming at first, it's just five $1,000 contracts or two $2,500 contracts.

## How to Create Packages and Pricing

Start with the underlying value of the item out of the gate: This is your starting point for what you'd charge before any bells and whistles like phone calls or upsells are added. Next, add in your time expected to complete that piece of the project.

If you're a white paper writer, for example, the writing isn't the only part of the project. You might have to interview people at the company before you draft an outline. All these smaller steps must be factored into your time. If you're a voiceover artist, it might take you multiple takes to get your performance right. Make sure you've included a fair price for your time.

Most freelancers don't provide enough detail at this stage of the project. You don't need to go into specifics, but you should provide information about the basic tasks it will take to complete the assignment. Here's an example, using the case of the white paper writer above: "This rate for one white paper per month includes up to five company representative interviews, transcription costs for those interviews, a drafted outline for approval, and two rounds of revisions."

Think about your time beyond the actual production of the piece:

$ Will there be back and forth with the client?
$ Will the client help with certain aspects of the project?
$ Do you have to find and read some unique piece of research or learn a new piece of software to do this job effectively?

All those details should impact your price.

Don't forget areas of special focus: Are you an expert at a piece of software used in the project that is hard for other people to grasp? Make sure you've charged accordingly.

## Offer a Minimum Package

There are time expenses in getting to know and onboarding a new client, and minimum packages help reflect what your time is worth to learn about their industry and their needs.

A minimum package is the bare minimum amount of work you're willing to do for any new client to make it worth your time to learn more about them. For example, a minimum package for a VA could include 10 hours of work per month with a 30-minute phone call. For a writer, it might be at least two blog posts. These minimum packages also work well as test projects when you have a new client who's nervous about working with you. Use the minimum package to knock their socks off and then move them into a more expensive offering. Over time, you might raise your minimum package from $500 to $1,000 and increase incrementally as it makes sense.

## Should I Use All-Inclusive Packages?

You shouldn't offer all-inclusive packages unless you have explained clearly what your boundaries are. I use an all-inclusive package for my coaching for freelancers. They get unlimited workweek business-hour support from me over Voxer, a voice-messaging app. That doesn't mean, however, that they can send me 30 messages a day and expect to get 30 responses. I set expectations upfront in my sales process and the intake call to make sure that they intend to use Voxer appropriately, would really benefit from this unlimited coaching, and understand typical response times.

## Upcharge for More Difficult Clients

You can even develop packages based on how easy the client is to work with. A client who doesn't need a lot from me is going to get a low-touch package, but with better pricing than the person who needs a weekly phone call. This is where sample projects are great for knowing how a person works in advance.

## How to Apply Urgency and Deadlines with Packages

When sending over a proposal, don't let the client think your pricing or turnaround time is good indefinitely. Add a deadline to the proposal to give them a reason to act.

Applying urgency is very important with packages. The concept of how harmful uncertainty can be with clients has come up a few times already. If you send a package proposal without a clear timeline for taking the next step, you might never hear from them again. A lack of deadline for your offer tells the prospective client that there's no need for them to lock it in today.

There are four main ways you can apply the concept of urgency when proposing a package:

1. Tell the client that the package offer expires using language like, "This offer is good for the next 72 hours," or, "I can hold this rate for the next 30 days."
2. If it's a current client, tell them that if they lock in now on a longer contract, you'll keep them at the old rates. This works well when your rates are going up but you want to extend a benefit to your current clients.
3. Offer a limited-time benefit like an upsell or a cost savings if they pay in full.

4. If true, hint that you're close to being fully booked and can only guarantee your availability for the next week or two. Use a waitlist if you do end up fully booked; if you've prepared the client for the possibility that you might not be available if they wait too long and they still come back, they're obviously serious about hiring you. And a waitlist creates a sense of FOMO (fear of missing out)—your clients think you're a hot commodity and they want "in," too.

## Tips for Negotiating Packages

A proposal or package sent to a client isn't necessarily the last word. A client might want to negotiate the terms with you. As always, the most difficult thing to negotiate is price. Consider adding or removing elements from the package and making other adjustments while still protecting your boundaries on price. If the lowest-level package is still too expensive for them, you might have to let the client go.

Ideally, if you've asked the right questions on the sales call and used that information to create your proposal, you won't need to do much negotiation.

## Understanding Hourly Packages

Let's talk briefly about creating hourly packages. An hourly package can be done on retainer, but it can also be done as a set of hours. The main difference is that you're getting paid by the hour rather than getting paid for each individual deliverable. These packages can be a little tricky, but you always want to give your clients an incentive for purchasing more with you. So if you are a virtual assistant, project manager, editor, or other freelancer who works on an hourly basis, you can still give the client incentives for purchasing more time with you.

Blocks of hours work well for hourly packages. When offering an hourly package as a block of hours purchased, you'll need to clarify whether unused hours roll over month to month or yearly and how clients can purchase additional hours if they run out.

For hourly packages, consider bonuses, discounts, or upsells for a client who chooses one of the higher-tier packages. For example, you might throw in an extra hour, a lower hourly rate, or a 20-minute strategy call.

When doing hourly work, it's important to give the client a general idea of how long certain projects might take so they aren't surprised when you use up all of a ten-hour retainer. For example, if it takes you roughly 3.5 hours to research and write a 500-word blog post, you can give the client a ballpark estimate of five hours to accommodate unforeseen issues associated with the task. Communication is key, and providing a general range is a good place to start. Another option that helps clients feel more at ease is to make some headway into a project for a few hours and report back with a better sense of how long the whole project will take.

It is far easier to go back to a client and ask them if they want you to proceed on a project that's more complicated than either of you expected than it is to send a "surprise" invoice after the fact.

## Mistakes to Avoid in Packaging

By this point, it's clear there are many advantages to packages: They're an opportunity to protect yourself, a chance to set the client's expectations, and a way to set the stage for addressing boundaries with the client. But there are three big mistakes you can make in your packages, including making yourself endlessly available, offering too much, or selling yourself as a jack-of-all-trades. Let's look at each of them in turn.

### *Endless Availability*

I strongly advise against ever including in the proposal or contract that you will be reachable (whether via Skype, WhatsApp, text message, email, or phone) whenever the client needs you.

You can (and should) specify your availability and response times in your packages. Maybe your VIP clients who invest at the highest level get 24-hour turnaround—meaning that if they send you an email, you will respond within 24 hours. For your non-VIP clients, perhaps it takes 48 hours for you to get back to them. This offer doesn't really cost you anything, but it's an easy upsell for a client who might want constant access to you, so consider their pain points when deciding whether to include these terms.

And even a two-day turnaround might have worked really well when you had three clients, but when you have ten? Not so much. New clients are a good opportunity to start clearing out old package concepts that aren't a good fit anymore—and that starts with your time.

### Offering Too Much

Remember how clients with too many options will take no action at all?

Don't offer too much to prospective clients. Don't say, "Here are the 100 things I will do for $500," because you'll end up being taken advantage of. Instead, offer a la carte items and increase your price as the job expands. For example, you could tell the client, "This package includes five social media posts. If you really want six or seven, we can discuss that and I can adjust the package for you." But don't offer too much just for the opportunity to work with a client.

### Jack-of-All-Trades Positioning

Freelancers who advertise that they can "do it all" tend to attract a certain type of client. I call them "manic clients." These people are totally frazzled and want you to fix everything in their business and life, and they usually go after people who position themselves as a jack-of-all-trades.

What happens next is that the client dumps a million projects on the freelancer, who doesn't have time to handle them and ends up doing a mediocre job, resulting in a disconnect and a breakdown between them and the client. So don't promise you can do "all the things" in your packages. Focus on what's most important and what you do best.

## Leveraging Retainers

Not every client is the right fit for retainers, but when you can transition someone over to an ongoing three-month or six-month working relationship, you not only get the benefit of regular revenue, but you also get the chance to know the client better and to continue striving toward goals together.

Most freelancers build their business with many different one-time clients. While there's no shame in working on one-time projects, the more you can shift to a retainer model, the easier it will be to predict cash flow and to deliver amazing long-term results for your clients.

In a retainer model, the client pays a flat fee per month based on the expectation of set deliverables, hours, or a hybrid of both. Think of them like a subscription model: Each month, the client will receive something they paid for in advance.

In the client's mind, there must be a reason for you to do work on an ongoing basis. If the client only needs a one-time website upgrade from a web designer, you might offer a one-time package for the list of improvements they've already given you and the opportunity to roll into a maintenance or smaller retainer after that. Hearing what the client needs and being able to recommend strategy are essential for retainers.

## Where Retainers Make the Most Sense

Retainers are a natural fit for work that needs to be completed on an ongoing basis. That includes:

$ Podcasting
$ Developing website content like blog posts
$ Social media management

Plenty of clients are overwhelmed by ongoing projects and content development, which is why so many of them are happy to hand over the reins.

That's not to say you can't be successful in offering retainers with other services. It comes down to how you package the need for the client to sign a contract for three months or longer.

Longer projects, like ghostwriting a book, can also be broken down into monthly retainers to allow for milestone delivery over a longer term. A client might not have the upfront budget to pay for the entire book, but they could schedule to pay for and review one chapter per month for a year.

If you currently offer a service that makes for a great one-time offer, like writing an "about" page for a website, consider how you can expand into new related services while delivering consistent value. Having a series of smaller retainers with services that are friendly to ongoing work can help someone like a web designer offer an affordable option for plugin maintenance and site speed tests—work that doesn't take a lot of time but is something plenty of webmasters and site owners don't want to worry about.

## The Freelancer's Guide to Following Up

As an experienced freelancer, you already know that most deals are not closed with a simple phone call or an email pitch. Just like it takes time for you to be comfortable with a company, product, or service, some of your clients might require multiple touch points to build trust and decide to work together.

Whether you pitched a retainer or a one-time package, it can take some back and forth to negotiate details, for the client to think over the offer, and for them to consult with anyone else in their company who might need to sign off on the project.

With previous or future clients, following up is essential. People are constantly bombarded with information, advertising, and notifications. To stand out, you must be willing to continuously follow up with your clients.

For a sample follow-up schedule, see the resources page on the website for Handout #16.

### Following Up After a Pitch

After you send a pitch, check in several days to a week later if you've received no response. Remember that your clients are busy; they probably won't have read an email you sent yesterday afternoon. Give them time to digest and if your email hasn't been opened yet, consider reaching out via an alternative method like LinkedIn.

When following up, make your next message unique. "Did you see my message below" or "Following up" add no value for the client and come across as spammy. Look for more personalized ways to continue the conversation, such as complimenting something the company recently did, mentioning a news story about their founder or a study that's relevant to their industry, or something else that stands out and calls attention back to your pitch.

Below are several ways you can follow up based on your last interaction with the client.

### Following Up After a Phone Call

The follow-up to your initial phone conversation or pitch should happen as soon as possible after the call. Give yourself time to digest the conversation and write up your notes, and then circle back with the client while the information is still fresh in their mind. This follow-up should be in the form of the proposal, including the work, the recommended deadlines, and your pricing.

In your follow-up, make direct points related to the call. "As you mentioned on the call" is a perfect way to lead into your recommendations. If you're spending more than two hours on a proposal, you're either overthinking it or you didn't ask the right questions on the phone call. Be ready to show them your offer in a timely manner.

Here's a sample starting point for your follow-up, but remember to personalize it: "It was great speaking with you. I'm writing back to send along my proposal, as promised. Looking forward to discussing with you—please let me know if you have questions or would like to connect in X days to discuss."

### Following Up After a Proposal

After you send off the proposal, give the client a little time to review it. Much like the email, they might need a few days to even notice it, much less pass it on to other team members who need to review it. Attaching a deadline to your proposal sets you up perfectly for a follow-up opportunity. Circle back after a few days if you haven't heard back, unless the client has told you otherwise.

After sending a proposal, reiterate your interest in working with the client. You can also stay in touch with them organically by not mentioning the proposal as the lead point. For example, perhaps you're a graphic designer who makes infographics. If you come across a new study about the power of infographics or a great example of an infographic, you can share this with the client. Mention that you came across this find and wanted to share with them because you think it could be relevant for what you proposed, but you don't need to come right out and tell the client this. You might say, "I know we mentioned the importance of posting on LinkedIn in our last discussion; I thought you might find this study interesting." You don't need to add in a closing sentence about your proposal if you choose this organic route.

## Do Multiple Follow-Ups with Clients Decrease Efficiency?

No. Sometimes it takes a lot of interactions for a client to decide to work with you. I've had clients who only signed a retainer agreement after 18 months of follow-up. I build in reminders to connect with them every few months unless they tell me they will never need my services again. Keep closing the loop with potential clients—you never know when it will pay off.

---

### Winning Proposal Writing Tips

Getting to "yes" involves a lot of behind-the-scenes work on your part. You can get there faster with a proposal that shines. Writing a great proposal and package includes four key parts:

1. Start off your proposal with a warm greeting that reminds them of your conversation and draws a connection from that to a future where you're working together.

2. Recap some of the reasons you made your recommendations. This might include some additional statistics.

3. If the client was very clear on the call about what they want, reiterate this in simple terms in the package recommendation, along with your pricing and delivery. If the client is relying on you for additional strategy, recommend at least two and no more than three packages.

4. Recap the timelines you discussed on the call or came up with since the call and the next steps for them to take, as well as details about whether or not this proposal will expire.

---

## — CHAPTER SUMMARY POINTS —

$ Both psychology and strategy play into the development of packages and propos-als—use the pain points you know about your client from their messages and your call to create a proposal that fuses their concerns with your strategic recommen-dations.

$ Clients who are confused or overwhelmed take no action. Present packages that have clear recommendations, empower the client to make their own decisions, and represent the best deliverables for their individual needs.

$ Be prepared to follow up several times, if necessary. If you're sending a lot of proposals and not landing the business, you have an issue with clients, pricing, or the proposal itself. Workshop these materials or hire a coach for a strategy session to figure out where your problem lies.

### *Resources Mentioned in This Chapter*

$ Sample Follow-Up Schedule, Handout #16

# running your business like a ceo

D o you think of yourself as a freelancer or as a CEO? A freelancer sees themselves as part of multiple teams but might have trouble seeing themselves as a business owner who drives decisions with experience, data, and company policy. A CEO focuses on the long game by improving methods and processes to amplify results. To become a six-figure freelancer, you have to think like a CEO in the way you communicate about your business and in how you decide to spend your time.

Have you ever met a really smart CEO? Or heard one speak on a TEDx talk or podcast? They're savvy. They know their audience. They're good with people. And they're often masters of human psychology and how it plays into all aspects of business.

Stepping into the CEO role for your own company requires you to do the same. There are plenty of business tactics you can use, but many of them boil down to basic human psychology and the way people think, perceive you, and make decisions.

In this chapter, you'll learn more about increasing conversions, setting boundaries, and communicating with people that will help you get comfortable with your role as the CEO of a growing six-figure freelance business. Let's break it down into five phases: owning your rates, increasing conversions, capturing pain points, controlling your finances, and setting boundaries.

## Phase 1: Owning Your Rates

Setting and raising rates are often trigger issues for freelancers—a hot-button topic that most freelancers don't want to talk about. Claiming CEO ownership status over your numbers will help you feel more confident, nail your sales calls, and only attract and work with people who see your value.

It can be nerve-racking to quote a new rate that takes your experience into account, but you should never feel bad about claiming what you're worth. It's a common challenge even for advanced freelancers, but the more confidently you quote, the better you'll feel about doing it.

As six-figure freelance search engine optimization (SEO) expert Derek Jacobson said, "Set your rate and stick to it. Don't lower it just to land a job. Never take on a client that asks you to work for a lower rate on a trial basis." Freelancers often negotiate themselves out of a good rate before the client even has an opportunity to provide feedback. Freelance project manager Alexis Gilbert echoed this, noting, "When you say your number to the client, don't fumble or explain why. Just say it. The right clients will pay your amount. The clients who won't pay are also the ones who won't value your time, work, or energy."

Don't be desperate. I know it's tempting to say "yes" to every project that comes your way and, in fact this might be how you build your business initially! However, you can't scale your business by agreeing to work with everyone you meet.

Freelance writer Cyn Balog said her perspective on project acceptance and pricing shifted as she scaled: "When I started, I accepted all these jobs, even though they were under my pay scale, just because I wanted so desperately to make this work. But I was working all the time. Eventually, I learned to ask people to pay me what I was worth, and they responded. Now I don't work all the time. I have plenty of time off for vacations and family. And I make pretty much the same salary I made when I first started. Don't be afraid to ask for more, especially when you've been working with a client for a while."

Think about situations when you feel tempted to offer a discount or accept a lower rate. You might be able to tap into a limiting belief and figure out why you're even tempted.

## Claim Your Payment Terms Like a CEO

In addition to refusing to accept lower rates, you also don't have to agree to payment terms you don't like, such as waiting to receive payment in the mail or 30 days after you submit the work. As writer Nicole Rollender shared, "When I first started my business, I worked hourly for some clients, others per project/piece of content. Most clients sent me a snail-mail check after the work was long completed and in their hands. Three or four months in, I knew that if this business would be my main source of income, I needed to ensure my cash flow. I switched over to monthly retainers (at first, they were three-month commitments, now they're six-month commitments), where I received in-full, upfront payment electronically. For one-off projects, I either receive full payment upfront or will sometimes ask for 50 percent upfront and 50 percent immediately due upon completion. Most clients are totally willing to agree to these terms, and I've banished my cash-flow woes."

You get to decide what your ideal payment terms look like. Some freelancers want 100 percent payment upfront and would never deviate from that, while others might accept an offer to get paid 30 days after the work is finished if it means a chance to work with a nonprofit they love. Decide what your boundaries are.

## Phase 2: Crushing Conversions

One of the most important things to focus on as you scale your freelance business is increasing your conversions. Freelancers often try to increase their marketing efforts and try out new options when they should be narrowing in on those marketing options that are most likely to convert for them (if you read Chapter 5, you should have already done that). When you identify your zone of genius with regard to converting clients, you can start earning more by doing less.

Conversion is all about efficiently achieving your optimal client or project load with a reasonable amount of pitching or sales time. If you're consistently spending a lot of time on the phone with prospective clients without converting them into one-time projects or retainers, that's a big upfront investment of your time with no return. If you can refine your process for screening and speaking to clients, by the time you get on the phone with someone, there is a good to great chance that they'll be interested in hiring you. Similarly, most aspiring six-figure freelancers have a well-honed process for sending pitches because they know those pitches are likely to convert—or at least lead to a conversation with a prospective client.

On face value, most freelancers want to skip improving their conversion strategy, assuming it's just a question of finding more clients. But if you reach out to 100 people and end up doing business with none of them, you're just wasting your time. Conversion is about getting more work by doing less.

### Defining a Conversion Strategy

Conversion strategy is about efficiency—earning more and doing less by bringing in more ideal clients and converting them in higher numbers. But it's also about finding the optimal project and client workload in a reasonable number of pitches. Logging 100 hours blindly sending out pitches that go nowhere or in landing a couple of small clients is a losing strategy. Even a fully booked freelancer needs an optimal conversion strategy because they might only have five or ten hours a week to spend converting clients.

If you spend a few hours researching a client, pitching them, getting on the phone, and writing up a proposal that turns into a retainer for a few months of work, that's time well-spent. A freelancer with a multifaceted marketing approach looks at all the options on the table, tests what works, and makes minor tweaks and upgrades to an already-working strategy.

For a business owner currently making a few thousand dollars per month who isn't fully booked yet, it might not seem like a big problem to spend 20 hours on a pitch and proposal for a new client, even if it doesn't convert to a paying project. But don't adopt bad habits early on. View this as an opportunity to test and refine your strategies, and it will pay off in the future.

## Recognize Your Nonbillable Hours as Part of Business Operations

Whether you have ten hours a week because you're still in your full-time job or 40 hours a week to build your business, not all those hours will be spent on revenue-generating activities. In a dream world, your hours would be primarily taken up with client projects, and you'd spend a limited amount of time pitching and completing administrative work.

There are plenty of nonbillable hours built into a freelance business: administrative work, answering small emails that you're not charging the client for, doing the legwork to write a proposal, or even hiring a business coach to help you refine your processes. Ultimately some of those things will lead to making money, but in the short term, there's no charge on the clock for doing them.

So a freelancer with ten hours per week to build their business might only have eight free hours to knock out client projects, spending the other two on marketing and admin. These hours should be used as effectively as possible to ensure they're helping you make money in the future.

Let's say you typically charge $50 an hour, and you spend a total of five hours researching a company, sending in a pitch, creating custom samples, and then scheduling a phone call with the client. The pitch ultimately goes nowhere. That process essentially cost you $250 because you could have spent that time working on a billable project at $50 an hour.

It's not a complete loss, because you learned something in the process, but you want to have as few of these experiences as possible. If you're consistently putting in a few hours a day with no results—in the form of signed contracts from clients—you're getting a poor ROI, and something in your process is broken.

### *How to Find Your Broken Pitch Point*

If you're sending out a lot of pitches but getting very little in the way of results, you need to figure out where in the process things are breaking down so you can step in and fix it.

You have two options to fix your pitch situation. First, you can reduce the time spent per pitch so that you can send more in less time. The other choice is to land more of the gigs you do pitch. Bonus points for doing both.

Bear in mind that no one has a 100 percent conversion rate. Occasionally I've had freelancers ask me what an ideal conversion rate is; there's no one answer. It depends on the platform, the time of year, and the service, among other things. If you send out ten pitches per week and you're lucky if one person even reads your email or writes back, you'll need to increase your pitching if you've already done everything you can to tweak your pitch.

Very rarely will a client open your email/Upwork bid/LinkedIn message and respond with a ready-to-sign contract. With more than 300 clients on Upwork, I've only had two people hire me outright without talking to me first, either through email or over the phone. The pitch isn't about getting business; it's a conversation opener. A pitch leads to a phone call, which likely leads to a custom proposal for that client. The phone call also helps the client see and hear you as a human. That's when they confirm that you're an expert and decide whether they like you.

To get a sense of where you stand with your conversions, use a spreadsheet or a CRM program. Record when you sent the pitch, how, the date you had a response or phone call, and your next steps. Use color coding: green for booked business, yellow for a warm lead, and so on. Looking at this data, you'll start to see where your process is falling short. Are people never getting back to you at all from your first pitch? There's a problem with the pitch, the pitch method, or the kind of clients you're targeting. Do you never hear from people after you send a proposal? Maybe you can improve your followup or clarify the pricing in your proposals. The goal here is to figure out what part of the process or parts can be fixed.

Unless someone directly tells you they never want to hear from you again, don't delete them or redline them in your spreadsheet. Even clients who say no now may be interested in working with you in the future.

I have distinct pitches for every different type of service I offer. They all touch on the same general points about my personality and my work, but they're different because the work I'm pitching is different. If you're doing a bunch of Upwork pitching, you might have the Google Doc or the Word document with that pitch open; copy and paste it into the Upwork mainframe and then make tweaks as you need to.

Make it easy for clients to book a time to speak with you. Don't rely on the back and forth of "How's Tuesday?" Instead, provide them with a link to book or make a specific recommendation off the bat, like, "I've got 1 to 4 P.M. Central open on Tuesday. Any chance you've got 15 minutes in there?" Tools like Calendly are free or affordable and allow you to set up a meeting booking link that syncs with your calendar.

## Phase 3: Creating a Template Pitch and Adding Client Pain Points

When people read your pitch, they go on a psychological journey. You're walking them through what it would be like to work with you. So if you have standard offers, like packages or a couple of different specialized services, this is a perfect opportunity to write a template pitch. Then you can map out the key things that you feel you have to touch upon based on your personal conversations with the client.

Clients will tell you what their issues are, either in an Upwork job post, a phone call, or an email. But they won't always tell you upfront—often you'll need to ask.

On an initial phone call, you can ask why they haven't outsourced the project yet. Was someone managing it in-house? Was another contractor hired who dropped the ball? All this is important for you to know since these details can be used to direct the remainder of the conversation.

When the client answers, listen carefully to the words they use to describe the situation: these are their pain points. Here are some common examples of pain points for freelance clients:

$ A personal lack of time to complete the project
$ A lack of interest in finishing the project on their own
$ Distrust in hiring someone online

$ Fear that you won't "get" their brand

$ Feeling overwhelmed

Any of these pain points should guide the rest of your conversation. For an overwhelmed client, for example, talk in your pitch or on the phone call about how simple you'll make things for them by breaking down the project.

If a client says, "We've hired other freelancers before and it's been a disaster," mention that you have a strong track record with other clients and reassure them with some of your social proof in the form of testimonials.

When you can capture these pain points and repeat them back to clients during a verbal conversation or in your proposal, it makes your proposal sound much more personalized. It also gives the client a sense of confidence that you listened to them and that you specifically understand their needs. Keep digging for more details if the client seems hesitant to give you the information you need to address these pain points.

## Dealing with Objections from Potential Clients

Pro tip: Be prepared for objections well in advance. You don't need a memorized response, but have some ideas drafted out on paper or your computer screen.

Common client objections include:

$ It's too expensive.

$ I'm not ready yet/this isn't a high priority right now.

$ This whole process confuses me.

$ I'm speaking with other freelancers.

Here's an example: If a client has already hinted you might be out of their price range, turn this around on the phone call. While you'll always be too expensive for some clients, stand firm in your value and reiterate that while they might have hoped for a rate that a beginner would charge, you have X years of experience and charge accordingly. Inform the client that you're a premium provider and charge rates higher than the industry average. Make this point and move on.

When you're confident in responding to these objections on the spot, you're leading with your value. You know what you're talking about, and you handle their objections with ease. This gives the client a glimpse of what it's like to work with you.

## Master Sales Calls

Are you worried about sales calls? Treat them like a CEO would and hop on these opportunity calls with confidence. Showing up to be of service to a potential client positions the call as an opportunity for all parties involved to take their relationship and results to the next level.

To start with, begin the call with some opening questions so you can learn more about their business. If you already did some research, warm them up with a complimentary statement about something you liked.

Let them know that the phone call is a chance to learn more about each other and see if there's any potential to work together. This prevents you from coming off as too eager. Gather the information you need from the client to write a great proposal and address their goals, concerns, and past or related efforts. Ask them who they admire so you can brainstorm similar strategies.

You might be thinking, "But Laura, I am a designer. Or a developer. I don't do sales." You absolutely must do sales because the business of freelancing is one of selling yourself and your services. If you're scared of sales calls, you can stick to marketing methods where you never have to speak to other humans. But you'll also limit your income potential. CEOs are are rarely going to be swayed by an email alone.

The world is filled with incredible resources on how to become better at sales. If you know sales is your weakness, start checking out some of those resources. For example, I often do 30-minute mock sales calls with my one-on-one coaching clients. In the call, I act like the most challenging sales call client: difficult, vague, and untrusting. After the mock call, I give personal feedback so they know how to improve their pitches. Getting over your sales call fear with a freelance friend or with a coach is a great way to improve your sales quickly!

I love reframing new client calls as "opportunity calls" rather than "sales calls." It removes some of the pressure for me in feeling like I have to "sell" and makes it more of an even playing field to see if the client and I are the right fit. If that helps you, please use it!

Here are some tips for leveraging psychology in your opportunity calls:

$ If the client found you, let them lead the conversation. If there's an awkward silence, ask them why they were drawn to you or how they found out about you. Then draw them in with a question about their biggest need.

$ If you found the client, do your homework in advance. Be prepared to discuss what they are and aren't doing well in their current marketing/strategy.

$ Lead with why you're interested in the company. Do they have a great mission? Do you use their products or services? Even if you already included this in your pitch, emphasize it again on the call. They might have read your message days or even weeks ago, and CEOs and marketing directors are busy. Remind them that this isn't a blind pitch—there's a reason you want to work with them.

$ Walk them through a series of questions. Some of my favorites: "Can you tell me what you've tried already that hasn't worked so well or has been hard to implement?" "Can you tell me someone else's strategy/vision/brand that you think aligns with yours?" "Who are your competitors? How are they different from you?" and "If you could wave a magic wand and change one thing in your [INSERT FREELANCE SERVICE HERE] strategy in 60 days, what would that be?" These questions give you a lot of information that will help you direct the remaining conversation.

$ Remember that the call isn't about you. Clients just want to know that you're qualified. The rest of the call should be about *them*. Only talk about yourself in the context of how what you do and the way you work solves *their* problem.

$ Avoid giving pricing information on the call. Tell them you're taking notes and that you'd like to follow up with them either later that day or the next morning with a recap and a custom proposal. Most clients are pleased that you create a proposal tailored to their needs and will be willing to wait.

$ Always know your UVP (see Chapter 4 for more on this).

$ Be prepared for objections and rehearse your responses to them before getting on the call.

$ Ask for information about their goals and reasons for outsourcing now to capture their pain points in their own words.

$ Stand when you take or place the call. It changes your energy and makes you feel more confident.

$ Remember to tell the client your next steps, such as writing a proposal for them, so that they know what to expect from you.

> Use this power-positioning statement in your call: "I'd like to write a proposal for you based on what we discussed. Once I have a chance to review my notes, I can get that to you this afternoon. Does that work?"

Even if you charge a standard hourly rate, do not commit to anything over the phone. Tell the client that you're going to take everything you've heard on this call, digest it, and come back later with a customized proposal. This means that you get a chance to let everything sink in, determine whether you missed any questions, and avoid leading with a price on the phone call. Very rarely will a client demand that you give them a firm verbal quote; if they do, it's a sign they might be difficult to work with or only care about price.

## Responding Professionally to Rejection

Every freelancer will hear "no," not just once, but often. It's the nature of the business. Even after you increase your conversions, there will always be clients who find you too expensive, too cheap, too experienced, not experienced enough, or just decide to go with someone else or do the job themselves.

It's sometimes tempting to get upset when this happens, but it serves no purpose. Remember: Don't burn bridges unless you have to. A client who rejects you now might come back to you in the future or refer you to someone else. Keep things professional and thank them for the opportunity. If they just weren't ready at this time, it's fine to ask if you can circle back to them a few months later. Beyond this, let it go. You don't need to continue following up with anyone who gives you a firm "no."

### *Don't Give Up Too Soon*

Often, in Facebook groups, you'll see newer freelancers crushed that an opportunity they were counting on didn't pan out.

Experienced freelancers know that no one job, client, proposal, pitch, phone call, or interaction defines them. In Chapter 6, I covered the importance of following up. If there's a line of communication open, keep following up. If the one project you thought was yours somehow falls apart, don't let it break you: pitch, pitch again.

### *Don't Close Too Soon*

Most people hate being cold pitched without any personalization or previous conversation. Going immediately into the sale rarely works. Each week I get hard sales pitches in my LinkedIn message box. I immediately remove the connection to that person and ignore their message. No one wants to be sold to right away. We may live in a digital world, but it's still all about real relationships.

Never go in blind without doing your research. Finding out whatever you can about them *before* you pitch increases your chances of converting them. If the company founder was just named on a "40 Under 40" list, mention that in your initial outreach. Look at the company's competitors. Research their current blog and social media to see what they're doing well and where there's room for improvement. These small efforts to better understand a company and its leaders will go a long way toward helping your outreach succeed (whether it's an email or a LinkedIn message) and set you up perfectly for a future phone call or pitch. Don't blow your chances by sending a blast message along the lines of, "Hi, I'm a writer. Do you want to hire me? Do you have any writing needs?"

## Phase 4: Claiming Ownership Over Your Finances

As a business owner, you simply can't afford to ignore the financial arm of your business, even if you have not been trained to manage it. Therefore, it's wise to develop relationships with financial professionals early on so that they will be available to advise you as your company grows.

At a minimum, you'll need:

- $ Clear monthly or quarterly freelance revenue goals
- $ A bookkeeping system or accounting software to track expenses and sales
- $ Invoicing software or a system that allows you to send out and monitor invoices to receive payment (or a bookkeeper who can manage this software for you)
- $ A relationship with a CPA or other tax professional who can advise you about the tax aspects of your business, such as whether you should consider moving to S corp status
- $ A relationship with a financial or investment professional who can advise you about the kinds of retirement accounts available to you (or some self-education on the subject)
- $ A system set up to capture the information you need to pay your quarterly taxes

If you're not ready to upgrade to paid relationships with professionals yet, keep a close eye on your finances. Take it from six-figure freelance writer and content strategist Seraine Berube, who said, "Taxes aren't as scary as you think. I absolutely detest math, so the thought of messing up numbers and potentially being audited for a silly math error really scared me into staying small with my business. For far too long I kept my earnings under $600 per client so I wouldn't have to try and figure out in-depth tax stuff. QuickBooks was a lifesaver for me. It kept me organized with sending invoices, paying estimated quarterly taxes, and generally just organized on the admin/money side of things. I'd also recommend an accountant as soon as you can afford one. They know the tax laws best so you won't have to waste your time figuring it out."

Know how the self-employment tax affects you and continue to discuss this with your CPA or other financial professional as you scale.

In addition to managing your business finances like a pro when it comes to tracking revenue and expenses, you also need a firm grasp of how much you should spend on things like software, website hosting, subcontractors, and more. The best book on this subject is Mike Michalowicz's *Profit First* (Portfolio, 2017), in which he provides excellent advice about how to make sure you pay yourself so you aren't spending too much on expenses. Most freelance businesses nearing the six-figure mark will not have many expenses, depending on whether the company is run as an agency or solo effort; 25 percent of gross revenue set aside for expenses is a good benchmark, although your numbers might be less. The Profit First methodology developed by Mike Michalowicz clarifies your finances in a way that's easily understandable and systematized. You can also use his method to determine what percentage of total revenue should be set aside for expenses based on project revenue.

Set aside time each week or every other week to review all incoming and outgoing cash flow. Doing this on a regular basis means you will spot problems earlier and maintain a consistent and positive relationship with your money.

For more information about freelancer finances, I strongly recommend Katelyn Magnuson at The Freelance CFO (www.katelynmagnuson.com). She has free materials and a Facebook group as well as online courses to help you make sure you never neglect your money!

## Phase 5: Nailing Your Boundaries Down and Honoring Them

Do you have a clear list of boundaries? Are there personality traits, business practices, or communication habits that you just won't tolerate in clients or ones that you'll accept but respond firmly to?

If your professional boundaries have been lax until now, consider this your official warning to tighten them up or you will continue to attract nightmare clients.

When you started your business, it was thrilling just to get a new client. The idea that someone would pay you for your work was exciting, and you felt lucky to have the opportunity. Shifting into a CEO mindset, however, means that you have to think more about protecting your boundaries so that you only work on the projects that serve your goals.

This requires airtight boundaries. These are not a "one and done" topic. You'll likely have to revisit them at least a few times, especially if you have a particular bad habit, like allowing overbearing people into your world or feeling like you need to please everyone.

Each freelancer has their own boundaries. For many people, it's unacceptable for a client to call or text on the weekends. But if you allow this early in the relationship, it's much harder to get the client to stop later on.

Setting appropriate boundaries is one of the biggest challenges for six-figure and advanced freelancers. Here are a few warning signs from clients that might indicate a need for firmer boundaries:

$ Pushing you to do more than you agreed to for no reason, because you've worked with them for a long time, or because they think they're paying you really well

$ Treating you disrespectfully, such as yelling at you on the phone

$ Demanding more revisions than the contract allows for

$ Getting mad when you don't answer emails or texts within five minutes

$ Expecting that you'll drop whatever you're working on for their needs

Because there are lots of important things to note about boundaries, there are three training videos on boundaries on the resources page on the website, www.sixfigurefreelancebook.com/resources. They include a deep dive into dealing with vague clients, clients who engage in scope creep (ramping up the amount of work on the project beyond what you agreed to, sometimes without pay), and how to enforce solid communication boundaries with your clients so they know how and through which channels they can reach you. You'll learn how to deal with each of these scenarios.

## Recognizing Toxic Clients

Sometimes even the best boundaries can't keep nightmares out of your business. Toxic clients happen to plenty of freelancers, and sometimes the best solution is a firm and quick exit.

A toxic client is someone who drains all the energy and life force out of you. They are overbearing, overwhelming, and demand lots of extra work from you, usually without more pay. They tend to provoke frustration and anger in the freelancers they work with, and can even cause you to feel burnout because they bring out the worst in you.

If you generally love working with your clients, it will be easy for you to spot toxic clients because of how they make you feel. If you have *only* worked with toxic clients it may take you longer because you don't know what behavior patterns to look for. A few questions you can ask to identify a toxic client are:

$ Does this person treat you poorly?

$ Does this person not pay you well?

$ Does this person always ask for discounts or a reduction in price?

$ Does this person make you feel like you don't quite deserve to work with them even though you are giving it your all?

## Toxic Client Red Flags

While you can't always identify a toxic client before you work together, there are some ways to spot red flags early.

$ *How do they talk about their past freelancers?* Ask new clients to tell you about their experiences working with freelancers in the past. If they tell you they have worked with 15 other graphic designers and they were all horrible, the odds of ALL 15 being awful and unprofessional are very low. Almost certainly there's something wrong with the client, not the freelancers. A few bad freelancers is OK, but large numbers of freelancers being considered "awful" is a red flag that you are dealing with a toxic client. (If they have never worked with one before, this could be your chance to show them how they should act, work with, and communicate with freelancers.)

$ *Do they expect you to be available 24/7?* These might be communication issues that cross your boundaries. A lot of times toxic clients will raise this themselves and say it's important for you to be available around the clock—that's the point when you know this relationship probably isn't going to work.

$ *Do they ask you to prove your worth?* A toxic client might push you to prove your worth to them even on the initial phone call. They might constantly talk about ROI. They may not be willing to sign a contract for more than a month because they just don't trust you. They might pay you 10 percent upfront and then the rest when they are "satisfied" with the completed product. This is a red flag.

$ *What are their communication preferences?* This is a huge issue. As a freelancer, you have to set boundaries with clients on how you can and will communicate with them. With toxic clients, always get everything in writing whenever possible. Communication choices for this include email, documents sent via email, text, etc.

## What to Do with a Toxic Client

If you realize you have a toxic client, call their behavior out as soon as it happens. For example, you have a call with a client, so now they have your number, and they start texting you at 10 P.M. First, you ignore the text. Next, you wait until business hours the following day and send them an email letting them know your phone is turned off after business hours and you will not respond to any texts sent outside that time. Encourage them to reply to the email with any concerns. Even with emails, don't respond until business hours.

If a client speaks to you unprofessionally, call it out in the moment as nicely as possible: "I don't know if you mean for this to be coming across this way, but . . ." Sometimes the client will apologize and say they didn't intend to be rude. This is when you have to make a judgment call about whether to continue the relationship. If someone is openly rude or swearing at you, don't even engage any further.

If you are in a relationship with a truly toxic client, you can't afford to keep working with them, no matter how much money they're paying you. First, if you calculate the actual amount of time you spend working for them, you probably aren't getting paid what you're worth. Plus, if you add in the emotional, mental, and physical toll they're taking on you, it's not worth it. They will burn you out. They will make you question your capabilities and so much more. Not only does it affect the work you are doing with them, but it could bleed over into the work you're doing for your other clients.

Navigating out of this type of relationship is tricky. First, try to let them correct their behavior. If they can't, then keep it professional and let them go.

## *Determine Your Company Policies Based on Your Boundaries*

Now that you know what your boundaries are, it's time to create some company policies and guidelines that protect your interests. This can be an internal document just to remind you of your goals as a CEO or formal policies that help you create proposals and work contracts.

There are many things you might want to include in your company policies, including:

$ How you'll handle unhappy clients

$ How many rounds of revisions you'll offer

$ What kinds of communication methods you'll allow for clients and whether you offer any specific guarantees, like a response within one business day

$ How you'll handle late invoices

$ If you're creating something with a copyright, like stock photos or written work, whether you'll maintain your byline/copyright on those products or sign it over to clients

Put your company policies in place before you outsource work to anyone else as a subcontractor or bring on someone like an executive assistant. This will greatly reduce the amount of time you have to spend bringing them up to speed on how things run in your business.

## —— CHAPTER SUMMARY POINTS ——

$ You need to claim ownership over your new status as a CEO and verify that all your company policies are in line with that, including your rates and finances.

$ Identify your current conversion rates and optimize your process to improve them.

$ Use pain points to drive all communication with clients before they sign.

$ Set and honor your personal boundaries and create company policies to match them.

$ Spot toxic clients as soon as possible and part ways.

### *Resources Mentioned in This Chapter*

$ 3-Part Training Videos on Boundaries

CHAPTER 8

# streamlining with systems and shortcuts

---

I f there's one word that defines a successful advanced freelancing business, it's *streamlined*. Looking for opportunities to improve their systems, relationships, communication, outsourcing, and more helps modern businesses stay adept and keep their spot in a competitive marketplace.

The big picture involves stepping out of the *doing of tasks* in your business so you can do more of the *strategizing*. That comes from a mix of streamlining and optimizing your current processes, focusing on the levers that move your business forward, and outsourcing administrative and lower-level tasks to other people.

In this chapter, you'll learn about some important aspects of establishing systems in your business that, when implemented correctly, can simplify your life and make it easier to bring on new clients and new outsourced hires.

## Setting Your MITs and Quarterly Rocks

Even though it's geared toward employee teams, the book *Traction* by Gino Wickman (BenBella Books, 2012) can also help solopreneurs and agency owners think about setting the right kind of goals using a concept the author calls "quarterly rocks."

Quarterly rocks are a way to streamline your focus and create clear outputs for accomplishing tasks within a 90-day period. I've found that with a little adjustment they are a perfect tool for growing your freelance business. Your quarterly rocks are generally broken down into biweekly or weekly tasks and then further broken down into the most important tasks (or MITs) that you work on each day.

### Making Use of MITs

MITs refer to your "most important tasks." On any given day, there should be no more than a handful of these. Some people prefer a maximum of five per day, but others find the sweet spot is three. The idea is not to overwhelm yourself with a list of ten things that you've determined are vitally important, "must-do" tasks for the day.

Getting distracted is a serious issue for many entrepreneurs, who are often full of ideas and love learning new things. This can be a dangerous combination when you have client work to do and want to expand your business. You don't have to shut down your pursuit of passion projects, but adding 15 new things to your plate can quickly become overwhelming.

MITs and quarterly rocks give you a sense of focus and help you recognize when something doesn't need to take up space in your brain or schedule *today*. If you suddenly have an amazing idea for a new book, marketing plan, or passive income source, brain dump it into a Google Doc or a Trello board for future consideration. Saving your ideas somewhere gives your brain a sigh of relief that you're not going to forget them, but it's also a good reminder that unless you need to make a major pivot from your MITs, you don't have to act on them right away.

You may believe that only focusing on a few goals at a time is limiting. I would love for you to be the exception to the rule. But time and again, I've seen scaling freelancers try to take on too much at once, fail, and then beat themselves up for being unable to meet their self-imposed deadlines.

Take one of my coaching clients. I'll call him Greg. When we first started working together, he felt as though he was making no progress at all. He was meeting his client deadlines but felt like he'd hit Friday afternoon each week and say, "Wow, I barely made it!" He wouldn't have updated his samples, revised his marketing, sent any new pitches, or finished anything else on his to-do list.

Our first week together, I asked him to choose his three most important tasks aside from client work and set those as his new goals for the coming week. These were not to be major goals, like "build a website," but rather tasks that contributed to some of his bigger goals, which he could realistically complete within a week. For his quarterly goal of launching his freelancer website, for example, his weekly MIT might be to post a job description for a website designer and start reviewing candidates.

Greg's first response when it was time to chat weekly goals was "I know you said three, but . . ." and then went on to name a laundry list of tasks he felt he needed to do within the next seven days. The list included finding a Pinterest manager, learning Pinterest himself so he could train that person, sending 35 pitches, and writing 5,000 words for a book he wanted to author. All these were lofty goals that had nothing to do with his quarterly plan to create a website. When I asked what progress he'd made in the past with similar goals, he admitted he hadn't written one word for the book or even outlined it yet, and that he was lucky if he sent one pitch a week. This is called setting yourself up for failure.

But Greg was adamant, so I let him run with this massive to-do list and checked in again on Friday. Not only had he completed *none* of the tasks he'd chosen, but he was also in an emotional tailspin because now another week had gone by and he felt like a failure. Overloading your to-do list and accomplishing none of it can be overwhelming and self-defeating. And 90 percent of it is self-inflicted. Slow, steady, and meaningful progress toward your goals sets you up to claim a series of small wins, rather than spiraling down at the end of the week as you stare at an uncompleted task list that was too big to begin with.

For the following week, we tweaked Greg's MITs to end up with the following:

$ Draft About page with snappy bio
$ Decide whether logo needs to be updated
$ Write and post job description for web designer on freelancing website

As he checked in over the week, I brought his attention back to these tasks again and again. They were clear, connected to his quarterly goal of launching a website, and a great starting point for reinforcing the concept so he could set his own MITs in the future. At the end of that week, he had accomplished all three goals and felt his website project was back on track. Better yet, he was thrilled with his progress and pleased that he hadn't tried to give himself 15 more things to do to make MITs sound more fun. Think about which three tasks you'd be so proud of yourself for completing that you'd enjoy a glass of champagne or nice food or relaxation treat at the end of the week. Even if you're not a drinker, the idea of Champagne Friday can be tweaked for your own purposes. Maybe a nice meal out with a friend or a yoga class would be a great way to round out the week and celebrate your progress on MITs.

Note: Just because something is a quarterly rock does not mean it must take exactly 12 weeks to do it. Quarterly projects often take somewhere between one and three months to complete. I regularly complete mine in six to eight weeks if the MITs are well-defined and ticked off each week. The idea is that sometimes you might run up against obstacles in one rock, but you can always push forward in your other quarterly projects. One week you might be focused entirely on one rock or you could be working on a few projects at the same time. There's enough clarity and flexibility to the system that after a few quarters, you'll be a master. Don't worry if you don't get it quite right the first time; you'll be in a better position to define your MITs and rocks the next time around.

## Using Quarterly Rocks

Quarterly rocks still work really well for solopreneurs to keep focus on your most important projects.

To get your creative juices flowing and to further emphasize the difference between an MIT and a quarterly rock, here are some previous quarterly rocks in my own business, with the weekly MITs for that project listed underneath it:

$ Rock: Hire new executive assistant
  - MIT: Draft job description
  - MIT: Post job in FB groups, notify referral sources I'm hiring
  - MIT: Draft test job and decide on pay for it
  - MIT: Evaluate initial applications, round down to top five and invite to interview
  - MIT: Interview top candidates
  - MIT: Review notes from interviews, conduct follow-up, make offer, notify others
$ Rock: Rebrand website
  - MIT: Meet with branding designer
  - MIT: Determine updates to logo
  - MIT: Draft list of problems with current website
  - MIT: Discuss list of problems with executive assistant, add new ones
  - MIT: Post job for website designer
  - MIT: Approve new branding colors, logo as final
  - MIT: Evaluate candidates for web designer job, finalized quotes from each
  - MIT: Hire new web designer to complete task
  - MIT: Give feedback on first draft of new site
  - MIT: Update all social media graphics with new branding info
  - MIT: Update branding documents in Google Drive
  - MIT: Schedule social media for relaunch day
  - MIT: Publish new site
$ Rock: Collect input from other six-figure freelancers for book
  - MIT: Contact all freelancers in my personal network who'd make for great case studies

- MIT: Determine what questions should be asked to get most helpful input for the book
- MIT: Create Google Form for *Six-Figure Freelancer* input
- MIT: Analyze form and make list of common themes
- MIT: Look at what kinds of freelancers are missing from the form; ask existing submitters to send me names of other people
- MIT: Get freelancers to sign release form to be published
- MIT: Collect addresses from all those who submitted to get them a copy of the book on launch day

When you only have a few rocks to focus on at a time, it's easier to break down those MITs into daily or weekly tasks, chipping away at your big goal a little at a time.

> If you want to make MITs sound even more fun, think about which three tasks you'd be so proud of yourself for completing that you'd reward yourself with a glass of champagne, a nice meal, a yoga class, or another treat at the end of the week.

## Putting the Right Systems in Place

Now that you know what you want to focus on, it's time to think about how you can best optimize the current systems in your business.

There are many different ways to streamline your business. In the initial evaluation of your current systems, processes, and strategies, you will identify several opportunities to speed up your process. A common concern for freelancers in this situation is whether they will sacrifice work quality or overall marketing quality and conversion rates. Certainly you should not rush through your work or automate tools and processes to the point that they are no longer effective, but it can be just as harmful to ignore opportunities to get faster or to streamline and become more efficient.

As your company grows, some aspects of running your business will become even more exciting. However, there will also be complexities at each new level that require you to take a step back and think about working *on* the business rather than working *in* it. Whereas operating from your personal email address and pitching clients on LinkedIn by yourself might have worked when you were a solopreneur with just a handful of clients, expanding your business requires strategic thinking about which systems, software, and other tips and tools you can use to streamline your day and continue to grow.

Curious about which tools I use today? Check out Handout #7 on the resources page on the website for a regularly updated Top Ten Tools I Use to Power My Freelance Business worksheet.

One of the things that caught me off guard about growing my business was how ill-prepared I was to operate at the advanced level. Instead, I learned the hard way about setting a lot of boundaries, making the onboarding process easier, and hiring professionals to help me with certain aspects of growth.

## Limiting Distractions

Now that you know what you should be working on, it's time to talk about some of those time suckers that pull your attention away from your most important tasks.

You'll get the most out of your time when you can eliminate or minimize distractions. The MIT and quarterly rock process will help, but we all fall victim to distractions like social media. If you don't feel you can trust yourself to stay focused, consider tools like Freedom (a mobile app for blocking distractions) or Cold Turkey Blocker to limit desktop access to websites.

Even business-related tools like email can be distracting. I uninstalled Gmail from my phone two years ago and have yet to regret it.

Here are some other tips to help you avoid distractions that can block your progress:

$ Turn off notifications during your focused work periods.

$ Put your phone on airplane mode or leave it in a different room when you need to concentrate on work.

$ Use your autoresponder to indicate to clients that you're not available because you're knee-deep in a project. This helps train them not to email you unnecessarily, sets expectations for responses, and reassures the client that you give this level of attention to all your projects.

$ Use the RescueTime tool for a week to track how you're really spending your time and then adjust your schedule accordingly. Scale back where you can and table projects that might be a better fit for a VA to your "possibly outsourced" Google Doc brain dump.

$ Inform your family and friends when your office hours are, and stick to them. Make it clear when you can and can't be interrupted.

$ Install Kill News Feed on your browser if you're addicted to scrolling through Facebook. It won't block the mobile app, but it blocks the news feed on the desktop version of the site.

$ Consider uninstalling your most distracting apps during work hours if you really can't stay out of them. The mindfulness of "Do I really need this enough right now to go through the hassle of downloading and signing in again?" can save you from yourself.

Knowing how you're most likely to get distracted is essential for making any of the strategies mentioned in this chapter work. Know thyself!

Distractions can come in many forms, from social media notifications to email to people, and all these interruptions pull your focus away from your MITs and your quarterly rocks. Look for opportunities to hack your own brain, like uninstalling the Facebook app from your phone or using a tool like Cold Turkey Blocker to limit access to certain websites during your focused work periods.

One of the most commonly overlooked sources of distraction is other people. Whether it's family members who don't seem to respect your closed-door policy or a client who keeps popping up in your inbox, these distractions cost you time and energy.

Energy vampires or people who create constant drama can be extremely draining for business owners to interact with.

As six-figure freelancer Jason Resnick noted, "Stop putting other people's fires out. Have a plan of attack for every day and make sure that you stay on path to that. It's the only way to move your business forward." If you're constantly getting sidetracked because your VA isn't doing things properly or simply because you're having a really hard time finishing a certain project, take a look at your emotional mindset and whether you can do something to get back on track. If you're bored by the project, for example, this indicates a bigger problem that you should address.

One of my coaching clients reported that she was distracted and "unable" to get work done for six days in a row. She was numb, bingeing TV for three to four hours a day and then beating herself up about it. This was a clear sign that something was really off. After ruling out the obvious (was she sick?), we realized it was a mix of not being excited by her business anymore and being scared that she wasn't experienced enough to take on her client's new project. Ultimately, the client decided she did not really enjoy working as a freelancer writer and instead pivoted to offer one-on-one coaching. While everyone has off days, watch for patterns that can help clue you in to bigger issues.

## Making the Most Out of Every Work Block

Have you ever decided to spend the day working on a project only to look up, realize it's 5:00, and wonder where the day went?

Meet Parkinson's law: the idea that work expands to fill the time available to complete it. If you've ever turned in a college paper 30 minutes before the deadline after staying up all night to write it or delivered work to a client by the "close of business" at 4:55 P.M., you know how this law works. What it means for freelancers is that we often give ourselves far too long to get something done, end up procrastinating through most of the work period, and then rush to meet the deadline.

Now that we can pass off much of the blame to Parkinson's law, meet the solution: the Pomodoro technique developed by Francesco Cirillo in the 1980s. We live in a very distracted world, and we're all guilty of multitasking. But there's plenty of research that shows it's actually holding us back; a 30-minute focused work session is more effective than a two-hour session in which you also check your email, take a phone call, and draft notes for a project you're not even supposed to be working on.

The main idea behind the Pomodoro technique is that several focused work sessions per day, each lasting 25 to 30 minutes, and separated by short breaks of 5 to 10 minutes, can actually help you get more done. (Some people prefer to use longer sessions of 45 to 50 minutes separated by short breaks.)

When I started playing with this technique, I was very resistant to the idea that 25 minutes was enough time to get any work done. But then

I remembered that for the entire first year of my freelance business, I somehow juggled clients, graduate school, and a day job. At best, I had 12 hours per week to devote to my freelance work, and somehow I still got everything done. The compressed time frame forced me to cut out distractions and get down to business. The Pomodoro technique works the same way.

When blocking out your day, resist the temptation to begin with five or six 50-minute sessions. Those can be hard even on someone very experienced with this technique. This isn't about cramming in more work across a 10-hour day. Choosing your top priorities at the beginning of each week or day helps you plot out how many focused Pomodoro sessions you need.

There are many online timers that will help you stay on track during your Pomodoro work period. To make use of ninja focus skills, however, consider investing in Focus@Will. The music it offers is tested to help you stay focused, and as an excellent bonus this tool has a timer you can set right within the browser or app. Leave it open in its own tab and get to work. There's a pleasant little "ding" at the end of your chosen work period, and you can choose from different channels like Water, Classical, or my favorite, Alpha Chill. I've been using Focus@Will on the Alpha Chill channel for so many years that I honestly think their 20 or so tracks are a signal to "get to work."

> Once you have a fair estimate of how long your tasks should take you, make your work sessions into a game. Set a timer and try to beat the clock or work from a coffee shop without your computer cord (bonus points if your battery power is under 70 percent when you start!).

## Setting Deadlines and Breaking Down Projects

One of the biggest challenges for new freelancers is determining how much time it will take them to complete a project. This can be especially difficult for new project types or projects in new industries. At the more advanced levels of running a strong revenue-generating freelance business, your concerns will shift to being able to juggle multiple priorities and deadlines at once. If you have scaled your company the right way by delegating and outsourcing to other professionals so you can remain focused on growing the business, you will also have an additional set of responsibilities: providing leadership and management to this team and strategizing the best systems and processes to keep all that organized.

In the middle of all this, you might overlook the importance of setting the right deadlines and breaking down projects. However, this is the perfect point in your business to make the intake, onboarding, project completion, and invoicing processes easier, based on the many projects you've already completed. A couple of small tweaks in the details can minimize the amount of time you must spend on these tasks.

Before you get started, it's helpful to look at the most recent typical project you completed for a client. Use a piece of paper to list out:

$ All the different tasks or sections of the project you had to complete
$ An estimate of the average amount of time you expect for each of those tasks
$ Underline anything that's already being outsourced to someone else on your team

Sometimes a tactic that made a lot of sense in the early freelance days just doesn't fit now that your company has grown. For example, if you used to promise two-day delivery to your clients when you only had one or two, this might be a good time to revisit whether that UVP is still viable now that you have more projects on tap. Setting deadlines falls to the freelancer most of the time unless the client has a specific endpoint in mind. By now, you should have a good sense of how long it takes you to complete projects so that you can accurately quote a client.

## Batch Work: The Game Changer

Batching your work (spacing the work out into different projects) is one of the most powerful tools for supercharging what you get done. It comes up so often as a challenge with my one-on-one coaching clients that the first question I usually ask is, "Are you already batching your work?"

Most freelancers don't start their business with batch work. Instead, once they onboard a client, they tend to work on that one project from beginning to end. Here are a few examples of what that might look like for different kinds of freelancers:

$ A writer will complete a kickoff call, analyze their notes, pick a topic or refine the client's selection, do research, write the piece, and edit it. Often this all happens over the course of one day!

$ A graphic designer might block out four hours to road map a client's new PDF from beginning to end. By that point they're so tired they shut down their computer and wait to finish another day.

$ A marketing consultant might go down the rabbit hole of analyzing a client's current performance in Facebook ads, then take a look at SEO, then review conversion notes from the sales team, all in the same working block.

Even though these are different kinds of freelancers, each with their own process and service, they have one thing in common: most clients have similar stages on their projects. And too many freelancers try to cram all the stages for one client into one long working stretch from beginning to end. One of my coaching clients once admitted to me that she spent nine hours writing one blog post over the course of a day. Her pay for that piece was low, and she finally realized that those nine hours were largely unproductive and anxiety-ridden due to the pressure (from the client and herself) to finish by the close of business. I advised that rather than setting aside an entire day for writing the post, she should have blocked out the pieces of the project and completed them over a series of days instead.

Decision fatigue is real. Over the course of a project, even if it's just one blog post, you have to make a lot of decisions as a freelancer. You also must jump in and out of many different kinds of work, like research and analysis, road mapping or outlining, the actual work, and revisions. This is why that client I mentioned above felt exhausted and frustrated that she hadn't completed more work. She'd asked her brain to do four or five different things on one day.

Let's use the blog post as an example of a job you could batch. If you're writing posts for several clients, each one might go through a similar process, regardless of the technical nature of the piece or the overall length:

$ Deciding on basic information, like the title

$ Completing research, like pulling links to use as on-page resources and outlining
$ Writing the actual piece
$ Editing the piece and submitting it

As a writer, I batch all my work. On Friday afternoons, I sit down and finalize all topics and titles for my client work that is due the following week or two. I don't start researching, writing, or editing. This does mean hopping around from one type of client to another, but I'm only asking my brain to do one thing: finalize titles and keywords. In one solid block of time, this allows me to complete a spreadsheet with all the relevant data I need to quickly outline and write the posts.

In another block of time the following week, I might spend three hours outlining for two different clients. Even though the topics are different, I'm asking my brain to do only one thing: outline. Another block of time is reserved for the writing process, and in yet another block of dedicated time, I edit those pieces and pass them off to my clients.

You might initially feel uncomfortable putting mismatched client work together. If you're building a website for a dog-sitting service and another one for a corporate lawyer, you might not think those site maps will look anything alike. But that doesn't matter—your brain is still focused on just one task, reviewing and finalizing site maps. Focus on moving forward and finishing a *process*, not an individual client's project.

Even if you're not a writer, there's a good chance that most of your projects follow a similar trajectory with similar subtasks. Building a process for this and slotting them into your calendar will make your workload easier.

To start, every Friday block out time in your calendar for the week ahead. Look at

> Once you get to Chapter 9, start thinking about which parts of your process don't actually need to be handled by you. In my experience, virtual assistants, once trained, are great at tasks like pulling resource links and proofreading. There's a good chance that you're claiming ownership over something in your process that you don't really need to do yourself.

how many client projects you have at various stages and which ones need to be moved forward in those phases. This is your road map to blocking out spots in your calendar for each of those phases. Use a tool like Google Calendar to reserve that time and then list which pieces of the client puzzle need to be completed during that batching block.

Here's a rough example of what this might look like for a freelancer over one day:

Monday, 9 A.M. to 12 P.M.: Complete research for three clients: Smithson, Quibly Electric, Backtrack

*Goal*: Accomplish outlines for all three projects, send additional questions to client on completion

Monday, 1 to 3 P.M.: Complete work for two clients, Markelson and Shah

Monday, 3 to 5 P.M.: Client phone calls, emails, and other communication with team

By blocking out the day into three batch periods, the freelancer is focused on only one task at a time. Each client's project moves forward, but there's also wiggle room if obstacles come up. If the research for Smithson reveals that the freelancer doesn't have enough information to continue, for instance, that project can be tabled until the 3 P.M. communication batched work session. In that case, the freelancer would instead spend the morning working on Quibly Electric and Backtrack.

Working in batches is less taxing for the brain, too. Even if you don't work traditional business hours or a full day, you can find a way to maximize your chosen work sessions with batch work.

To see a visual example of a batch work breakdown, check out Handout #7 on the resources page on the website.

## Setting Up Automated Processes

You can still provide a human touch to your clients while removing yourself from parts of the intake process that no longer require a personal response. Automated tools and software make it simple for you to capture the information you need and keep things organized while cutting out the need for phone calls, emails, or other unnecessary communication.

Let's say you've always held a kickoff phone call with every new client. Part of this phone call is used as a get-to-know-you conversation, but it's also probably where you asked plenty of questions about the client's goals, their previous efforts to resolve their current pain points, and any specifics they want you to file away in their instructions folder.

While it might still be helpful to have a kickoff call, you can streamline this process and minimize the time you spend on the phone by using an intake questionnaire that captures most of the details. The phone call then becomes about any follow-up questions you have and reiterating some of the most important information the client shared in the questionnaire. This is also an excellent opportunity to identify whether you are working with a client who has a lack of clarity about their goals and process. A client who rushes through the intake questionnaire or fails to provide appropriate responses should be an indication that you might need more of a hands-on approach.

There are some excellent automation tools out there like IFTTT (If This, Then That) and Zapier. Calendar tools like Acuity Scheduling or Calendly make it easy to connect your existing calendar with openings on your schedule so a client can book a call right away without any back-and-forth.

Here are a few places where automated processes make the most sense:

$ Sharing your new blog posts on social media
$ Reminding clients of an overdue invoice
$ Sending new prospects through a funnel with a lead magnet and an offer to get on a call with you
$ Sending out monthly retainer invoices on the same day each month
$ Asking new clients to fill out an onboarding questionnaire

To see an example of an onboarding checklist, check out Handout #8 on the resources page on the website.

## Automated Invoicing and Payment Follow-Up

Removing yourself as much as possible from the invoicing process will eliminate many headaches and can make it more likely that clients who are behind on their payments will get caught up. When invoicing reminders and notifications about late payment fees seem to be coming from an automated system or an email address that might be managed by a bookkeeper, a client who has fallen behind might get nervous about this information being shared with a third party and send in their payment as soon as possible.

Even though your efforts to send out and follow up on invoices might seem directly connected to billable hours, the work you're seeking payment for is already completed. Therefore, this is largely an administrative task that is not a good fit for your new business model, in which you operate as a CEO. You might even decide to outsource your accounting and bookkeeping altogether, but if you want to stay actively involved in the financial side of your business, there are still plenty of options to automate these processes with the right software.

There are a few invoicing software options out there; since company names or offerings might change, check out the bonus handout on www.sixfigurefreelancebook.com/resources to get the most up-to-date information.

### *Continuously Improve Your Systems and Automation*

Keep looking for opportunities to streamline and build your systems. When you notice that something is slipping through the cracks, that is the perfect chance to build a system or automation for it so you can avoid that problem in the future. If you've taken on too much, however, and your systems are completely disorganized or maxed out, this is when I recommend hiring someone else to help you with some aspects of your business—and that's where we're headed in the next two chapters.

## — CHAPTER SUMMARY POINTS —

$ Set goals and determine your most important tasks based on priority while not overloading yourself.

$ Cut out distractions any way you can so that your systems can accomplish what you want.

$ Work in blocks, break down projects into batches, and develop automations that capture repeatable processes.

## Resources Mentioned in This Chapter

$ Top Ten Tools I Use to Power My Freelance Business, Handout #6

$ Batch Work Calendar, Handout #7

$ Onboarding Client Checklist, Handout #8

# outsourcing to professionals

I t doesn't matter how fast or savvy you are, or how much you love control—you cannot manage a growing freelance business alone.

My outsourcing journey has been filled mostly with successes, but there have been some epic failures, too. Turning those into lessons for my life and business has helped me build my team and the teams of others more effectively in the future.

## Why You Need to Outsource

Listen to podcasts or watch video interviews or read books by the most successful businesspeople, and you'll begin to see a pattern in what they credit for at least part of their success: outsourcing.

But most people who have never handed things off to someone else panic when they hear the word. It can trigger all kinds of emotions because it seems scary to give up control over your work to someone else.

Let me introduce you to why outsourcing is so important and how it can help you make more money while having more time and mental space when you do it properly.

The first time I considered outsourcing, I had no interest in it. I had just moved to a new house that had a huge yard. We didn't have a lawnmower, and I was contemplating buying one and mowing the lawn myself. But one of my mentors at the time, who owned a website that got thousands of hits per day while managing an army of 12 volunteers, pointed out that I could have someone do it with their own riding lawn mower once every two weeks for $40, vs. the expense of buying the mower, paying for the maintenance and gas, and the two hours I'd spend mowing the lawn myself. My mentor said, "If you're making $50 per hour minimum with your clients, why are you giving up those valuable hours doing $20-per-hour tasks?"

That's when the lightbulb went on, and I haven't looked back since. I began an outsourcing journey that has taken many forms, from hiring my first virtual assistant to outsourcing all the writing in my freelance company to building and managing teams of outsourced workers for companies like TrueCar and Microsoft.

Along the way, the one key lesson I learned is that when it's done properly, outsourcing has the potential to change your business and your life. Some of the mistakes I made seemed like major failures at the time, but in hindsight, they were necessary for me to become a better business owner, manager, or person. Fortunately, I'm here to help you avoid as many mistakes as possible so you can outsource effectively in your business.

As virtual assistant Bai-Leigh Chapman said, you have to admit you need help and release your fear of losing control. She added, "It takes a village, so don't be afraid to ask for help or delegate when you need to. It can be hard to give up control, but it's necessary for success."

You will always feel nervous when you hire someone new or outsource a task for the first time. Give yourself time to adjust and reframe your hesitation by thinking about all the ways this new approach will help you accomplish your business goals.

Don't wait to hire help, either. Freelance copywriter Nicole Rollender shared, "Hire contract help as soon as you need it. I spent too long handling my own bookkeeping, invoicing, and calendar scheduling. As soon as I brought on an executive assistant (who turned into my business manager as I scaled), not having to handle those tasks freed up so much of my time to focus on CEO tasks like visioneering and marketing/selling. When it was time for me to hire junior writers to assist me with putting together client work, I also felt reluctant to do it, but I did it knowing the success I had in hiring an executive assistant, and it's paid off again in helping me scale and still have open time to be the CEO."

> "Delegate even though you don't feel ready. There isn't a time when you will feel ready. It is also what will get you to the next level."
>
> –Sarah Fox, freelance developmental editor

Remember, to work on the business, you first have to free up the time to do it. Virtual assistants are a great way to do that.

The first mindset shift that has to happen when you begin this journey is to stop thinking of this as an *expense* and instead reposition it as an *investment*. There are probably things you're doing in your business that:

§ You really aren't the best at
§ Take you longer to do than someone else would
§ Are not the best use of your time or don't generate revenue

Let's say you're a life coach, and most of your revenue comes from one-on-one coaching and your mastermind workshops. While there will always be elements of your business that you should handle (coming up with client homework assignments or writing blog posts, for example), there are plenty of other tasks that, put bluntly, *you have no business doing*. These may include:

§ Creating graphics for your welcome packet
§ Sending out emails through a newsletter/contact management system
§ Posting on social media

$ Answering FAQs that come in through email

$ Fielding public relations requests

$ Managing your calendar

$ Posting or formatting blogs you've written on your website

$ Managing your social media presence by connecting with new people

$ Creating an opt-in or freebie on your website to deliver value to clients

$ Posting blogs on your website or on LinkedIn to highlight your role as a thought leader in your industry

$ Invoicing

$ Following up with clients on unpaid invoices

$ Doing research for who you should be pitching (e.g., identifying the revenue, key players, and gaps in a company's marketing that make them an ideal client for you)

$ Proofreading materials you create, like client work, sample projects, and content for your website

$ Researching your travel plans

$ Identifying conferences or local events you should consider attending

$ Tracking analytics, such as the number of visitors to your website

$ Bookkeeping

It might ultimately turn out that only a few key tasks are in your zone of genius, like sales calls, showing up to coach your clients, and designing new programs. If you're new to outsourcing, this can seem way off in the distance, and that's OK. Once you get there you might decide that outsourcing everything outside your zone of genius just isn't for you.

For example, I outsourced all the writing in my business in 2015, and I was miserable. Clients complained. I found that I was spending hours on lower-level tasks that I wasn't good at and tasks that were not driving revenue. So I had to drill down and discover what I did best and what someone else couldn't easily replicate in my business. That came down to two things: talking to clients on the phone and creating the actual work. I had discovered that I *could* outsource everything but landing the clients, but I didn't want to, so I took back the writing portion of my business and focused on outsourcing the administrative work.

I share this story because I want you to know that how much or how little you outsource is up to you. It can change over time, but generally as you grow your business you'll need more outside help.

And herein lies the difficulty: Most entrepreneurs are used to doing things by themselves. While this may be because you start your business on the side while working a day job or because you simply can't afford any outside help in the beginning, you can rely too much on yourself.

These are some of the most common reasons I hear from entrepreneurs (even extremely successful ones with seven figures in revenue) about why they haven't hired anyone yet:

$ It's too expensive.

$ I don't have the time to train someone.

$ No one will get "my voice."

$ I've had a bad experience in the past.

$ I don't trust anyone else to do things the right way.

$ I'm very picky; no one will live up to my expectations.

To an extent, these are all valid reasons, but they are all based in fear, which serves no one. If you are truly happy with where your business is and have no plans to add new products or services, launch any new websites, or pitch new clients/customers, then you may not need to outsource. For most people, though, your business will naturally grow over time. If you haven't hit the ceiling yet, you will eventually.

The ceiling is the point at which you cannot do any more in a given day. It's your maximum capacity. We all have the same 24 hours in a day, and even with advanced productivity tips and working at peak efficiency, there's a limit to how much you can accomplish without sacrificing sleep, sanity, your family, and your health.

As your business grows, eventually you just don't have time to do the things you used to handle on your own. You may even notice that these tasks, which seemed "fun" or "new" at the beginning, are now a drag. If your customer or client base has grown, this has added new dimensions to your company, too, including more customer service emails, more technical websites that can carry more traffic and include more functionality, and more ways for you to keep up with your audience.

Remember the life coach above? Upgrading WordPress plug-ins and enhancing website speed are most likely not in their zone of genius—and they're certainly not revenue-generating. So if the life coach spends five hours a week fixing website problems, that's five $100, $500, or $1,000 hours that coach can't tap into.

## Making the Most of Your Revenue-Generating Hours

As a business owner, and particularly as a solopreneur, you're in control of two primary things: your time and your energy. You can't do anything about your time except work faster, focus more, or outsource. Even once you've applied all the ninja time hacks in the world, there's still likely to be a gap.

It all boils down to this: *As a business owner, you need to maximize your revenue-generating activities and hours.*

If those activities are sales calls and talking to your one-on-one clients, and you're doing as many of those as you can handle, you're eventually going to get tired, annoyed, and less focused. So by filling your only free hours with scheduling social media updates or other admin work, you're not just stressing yourself out, but hurting your clients and your conversions, too. Over time, you might even have to close your business due to burnout. If you're thinking it's too expensive to hire a virtual assistant or someone else to help you out, I'd argue the costs of not getting help are even worse—and potentially catastrophic.

Far too many business owners stay trapped under the time-bound ceiling for longer than they need to because they think they can do it all themselves. So they stay in this overworked, stressed-out state.

If that describes you right now, imagine what you could do with two extra hours per week. (The best way to get your feet wet with outsourcing is to start small, so for now picture two hours back on your plate.)

What would you do with that time?

$ More exercise?

$ More naps?

$ More sales calls to convert new clients?

$ Add one more client to your rotation?

$ Stop working a half-hour earlier each day so you could spend time with family or decompress?

$ Start that project you've tabled for months because you had no time to work on it?

Two hours a week might seem like such a small amount that it's not worth handing off to someone else, but that's clearly not true. Once you begin to see the benefits of outsourcing, you can start to feel comfortable upping a VA's hours or adding more people to your team. It's a bad idea to hire someone for 40 hours a week right away, but two hours seems doable. It might not revolutionize your life, but it might begin to show you why outsourcing is worth doing.

While from the outside it might look like I'm a time management ninja, there's no way I could get everything done without extra help. It took some time to find the right balance of outsourcing for me, but I can promise that when you find the way that works for you, you'll never look back.

If you're concerned that passing work off to someone else would trigger the control freak in you, you're not alone. Many solopreneurs don't want to give up control because they don't trust that someone else can handle the necessary quality or quantity of work.

But when people approach hiring someone from this fear-based position, it's a self-fulfilling prophecy. You're likely to wait to find help until you hit a wall with your own work and yell, "Fine! I'll hire someone!"

Then you race out and hire the first person you can find, either without an interview or with a five-minute Skype call. Then, once the assignment has been returned and it's poorly done, you tell yourself, "See? I was right. What a failure. This is a joke—I'm never outsourcing again."

If you approach outsourcing like this, with the mentality that they WILL fail, you're right. You're setting yourself up for failure.

It's a myth that you can hire someone, do no training, and expect them to get up to speed in one day. If that virtual assistant does exist, please tell me, because they're the holy grail of VAs.

## Having the Right Mindset to Outsource

Working with a virtual assistant is like many other relationships—it is built on strong mutual communication and trust. So if you're going into the hiring process not anticipating any work on your end, and you have zero trust because you already believe they will fail, is it really that rewarding to tell yourself "I told you so!" after they inevitably fall short?

There's a big learning curve to developing rapport with someone. It can take a few tries to find the right person to help you with your business—where the connection feels seamless and you can really begin to take a step back from the work. You shouldn't immediately put all your trust in the first VA you meet.

Instead, I encourage you to put a bit of trust in the *process*. That might look like this:

"I trust that hiring someone to help me is the right move for me. I might not get it right out of the gate, but I'm going to have faith that I can eventually find the right person or persons for me. I'll let my trust grow with people over time, but I'm going to trust in this process regardless."

Have you ever worked for a company where turnover was a major problem? I have. The first job I took out of graduate school was answering phones at an insurance brokerage, and on my first day, a co-worker said, "Good luck. No one has ever lasted a year in this job."

One year later, I handed in my notice. I had discovered on day one that they knew there was a problem, and they weren't going to do anything about it. The comment itself wasn't the reason I quit; it was the behavior they already knew was an issue. I was treated like I was replaceable, and they assumed I was worthless because of the company's past experiences with bad employees. It had become a self-fulfilling prophecy: They took it for granted that employees would leave, treated them poorly, and so they left.

Do you really want that to be you? Do you want to approach each hiring decision as a failure waiting to happen?

There is truth to the statement that "Good help is hard to find." But it's not impossible to find.

When you hire someone already believing they can't do the job, you've paved the road for them to fail. That's not a positive working environment for either of you. Eventually, like me, they will get fed up with being treated as if they're not valued and leave for some other opportunity.

Unless you have previously worked as a manager or team leader, it can feel strange to go from solopreneur to outsourcing pro. There's always room for growth in your management and leadership skills, and you will always learn new things along the way.

I found that I saw major improvements in my team's performance and relationships when I made the effort to trust them, to sit back a bit and see what the VA brought to the table. Time and again, this process has helped me discover the shining stars. I've also learned the value of the right personality. With the right people, you don't need to be a whip-cracking manager.

Just like with any other growing pains in your business, give yourself some room to make mistakes. Just learn from them rather than deciding you can and should do everything yourself. Those kinds of toxic beliefs lead to burnout and the same stifled business model that made you decide to outsource in the first place.

If you hire someone who isn't the right fit, that's OK—it's an opportunity to put on your manager training wheels and learn how to fire them. Choosing the right people and letting the wrong ones go will help you set boundaries with your business, your time, and your energy.

You deserve to enjoy more of your time and preserve your sanity. You deserve to watch your business grow effectively and become more of a business owner, as opposed to a "doer of things." Trust that this process can help you grow your company and make more money.

Remember, the right virtual assistant or other team member is an *investment*, not an *expense*. When they free you up to do more, better-paid, or higher-quality work, that's an investment that helps you increase your revenues. Could you do all this on your own? To a point, yes. But what if you could get there faster and as efficiently as possible? Outsourcing is the way to do it.

## Knowing What You Should and Should Not Be Doing

Once you have decided to outsource, it can seem like you've entered a quagmire of difficult choices. How do you know which tasks you can outsource and which ones you're better off doing yourself? Maintaining the right balance with outsourcing took me years to master, but in hindsight, there were a lot of things I could have done to make it easier.

First, take an audit of how you actually spend your time in your business. If your days all tend to look the same, this could be as simple as tracking what you do over the course of one workday. If you tend to jump all over the place, however, then it's better to keep track of your schedule for the whole week.

Whether it's for a day or a week, keep track of the time you spend on various tasks. These might include:

$ Creating content
$ Answering emails
$ Administrative work (paying invoices, etc.)
$ Scheduling blogs, podcasts, or social media
$ Client calls
$ Interacting in Facebook groups
$ Sending messages on LinkedIn
$ Responding to comments on your posted materials

As you go through your day or your week, write down how much time you spend on each type of activity. Track this in minutes and then tally it up at the end of the day/week. This might feel silly, but it can give you a real picture of where your efforts are going. A lot of people, for example, think that social media scheduling is quick and easy and therefore they can handle it themselves. Since you might be jumping on social media each day for a little while, you may honestly have no idea that you're spending up to five hours a week on the task. You might also be surprised when you take a deeper look at how you've been spending your time and how well that correlates with revenue-generating activities.

The reason that tracking your schedule for a week is so powerful is because you can see how every task, and indeed every minute, adds up over time. Once you have a full picture of where your time is going, you can make a plan for how you want to change that.

Ideally, you'll spend most of your time working on activities that are in your wheelhouse, that you enjoy doing, and that make you money. An activity that hits all three points is the trifecta.

But most business owners don't spend nearly enough time on these trifecta activities, and because of that, their growth is stunted. They hit an income ceiling below their maximum growth potential—but it's the most they can make with that particular strategy.

This exercise can also help you easily pinpoint things you don't want to or should not be doing. Let's say you discover that you are spending two hours per week scheduling your blog posts to go live. If you're posting once a week, perhaps two hours isn't that big a deal. But in the grand scheme of things, every hour counts. And what happens if you decide to increase your posting frequency? That's hours and hours down the drain.

Sometimes you need to see all those minutes totaled up to understand how turning over some responsibilities to someone else can free up your schedule for more revenue-generating activities or allow you to ease back a bit if you're feeling overwhelmed.

This is called the gift of time. When it comes back to you because you've outsourced some work, you get to decide how you want to spend it. Expanding your business? It's possible. Taking more time off to enjoy your life? Also possible. Learning a new hobby or starting a totally different side project from your current business? Yes, that's possible, too.

Once you've made your list and totaled everything you did in a week, try to determine which things you like doing best. Your highest-priority activity should be one that you a) enjoy doing and b) make money doing. For example, if you're an astrologist, most of your money probably comes directly from the calls you do with your clients.

Go through your list and circle all the activities you enjoy doing that also make you money *directly*. (You may think, for example, that posting on your blog or social media makes you money because it gets people into your pipeline—but when do your transactions actually happen?)

These are your key moneymakers, and it's in your best interest to use your focused, high-energy working hours on these tasks. This is not to say that the other tasks you work on are useless—they may in fact be important for your business, but they don't immediately translate to money.

The great thing about outsourcing is that it can work for you no matter what those tasks are. Perhaps networking in Facebook groups is a great use of your time because you actually convert clients directly through the Messenger app. If that's the case, focused time on Facebook may be right for you, whereas in most cases it's a really poor use of a freelancer's time, as most of their clients are not hanging out on Facebook, waiting to connect with them. That's why you need to do the audit exercise—to understand both where your time is going and where your money is coming from.

## Analyze Your Personal Results

Once you have identified how you're spending your time and what your key moneymaking tasks are, look over the list of all your weekly tasks and identify all the tasks you hate. That means the ones you dread doing, put off until the last minute, don't do very well, or rush through as quickly as possible to get them over with.

For me, this is web design and development. I know there are people out there who will say, "What do you mean? WordPress is so easy!" For me, it is single-handedly the biggest pain in my business to try to get everything functioning properly. I can easily lose hours down the rabbit hole trying to get a plug-in to operate or fix the fonts on my podcast page. And what a waste of time those things are. I end up spending twice as much time as I expect on the problem and still can't find a solution.

Then I head into my next task in a bad mood, convinced that I'm stupid and there's no reason I shouldn't be able to figure it out. There's no way continuing to work like that is effective. It's a very poor use of my time.

When you see the tasks you dread on your audit sheet, they are obvious candidates for outsourcing. If they don't make money, annoy you, and take a lot of time, transfer them to a new list, what I like to call my "stoplight list."

As you get used to outsourcing, you'll feel more comfortable handing over tasks to someone else. When you start out, though, you'll want to identify tasks simply and start off slow. Overloading a VA has all kinds of risks that could lead you back to square one, so avoid it whenever possible.

Your stoplight list categorizes tasks by how comfortable you feel giving them to someone else and in what order you want to do it. Take the tasks you hate the most and put them at the top of a list entitled "Green" if they can be easily outsourced (meaning that with a little training, a virtual assistant could pick them up pretty quickly and take over).

Ideally, you would move all your most hated and time-consuming tasks to the top of the green list, but that might not be possible. Think carefully about whether these tasks can be easily outsourced.

What's an example of a task that's not easily outsourced? Let's take podcast production or building a website. You might really want to outsource it, but it might be hard to hire someone to single-handedly manage that process for you right out of the gate. It would probably require a lot of training and explanation of your goals, your voice, your branding, and your expectations. At some point, it will definitely make sense for you to outsource those tasks if they are not in your zone of genius, but right now, the barriers to finding and training someone else may be too much for you to handle. Remember: Start small.

You might want to put these tasks on a "Yellow" list, to indicate that some steps are necessary on your part before they can be outsourced. "Red" usually refers to massive projects that take a lot of legwork before you're ready to outsource. You can continue to refine and come back to your stoplight list as you grow your business and increase your experience with outsourcing.

The most important lesson from this section of the book is that you need a way to get the outsourcing ideas out of your head and onto a clear list. Doing the work now to make sure you understand what you're looking for will make the process much easier as you move to the next stage— screening, hiring, and training your outsourced assistant.

As you look at the list, let's return to the idea of $20-per-hour tasks vs. $50-per-hour tasks I mentioned at the start of the chapter. Which of the tasks on the list can be outsourced for less than the ideal hourly rate you're earning doing revenue-generating activities? These are great places to begin considering outsourcing.

If you need more inspiration about the different kinds of tasks that virtual assistants can do, please check out Handout #9, Tasks Completed by VAs, on the resources page on the website.

Entrepreneurs find it really easy to argue, "But I can do all these things myself. That's how I've been running my business for years!"

I have no doubt that's true; however, if your business is going to continue to grow, you have to accept that you cannot keep doing everything yourself. You just should not be spending time on tasks that someone else may be able to handle better than you.

For instance, when I branched out from freelance writing into coaching and enrolling people into programs designed to help them make money online, I decided to teach myself how to use landing page software. It couldn't be that hard to design a landing page and encourage people to opt in to my list, right?

I was wrong. So wrong.

First of all, I know nothing about design. I know colors that I like in general, but beyond that, I'm not sure what works, what looks good together, and what will encourage someone to hand over their email address.

But I taught myself the basics, and I created a number of really hideous lead-generation pages. They were horrible.

They also didn't convert.

By insisting on doing it myself, I actually lost money in two ways. First, I spent countless hours trying to make these landing pages look right. There were always technical issues, aside from the visual appeal of the pages (which, by the way, was none). Then I got frustrated, and when I finally gave up working on them, I was in a foul mood. Furthermore, they converted so poorly that after a couple of weeks of watching my opt-ins slow to a trickle, I took every single page I had created down. Who knows how much money I lost from people who landed on the page and bounced off as quickly as possible?

This was a lost opportunity cost, and one it took me some time to recover from. But it taught me a very valuable lesson that was later highlighted again by my online business manager.

When she came on the scene, I didn't want to dump such a big task on her immediately—I wanted to give her time to grow into the role. After some time working together, I was ready to let her tackle a landing page.

She did it four times faster than I had, it looked professional, and all the elements worked properly. Why had I been so stubborn, thinking that I needed to do it just to learn how to do it? Considering all the hours and opt-ins I lost with my ugly design, that didn't help me generate any more revenue. If I had taken a fraction of the money it cost me in terms of lost time and opt-ins and given to someone who knew what they were doing from the outset, I would have been much better off.

Now, there are certainly situations in which you might engage in nonrevenue-generating activities just because you love them. Maybe your weekly Facebook Lives or your podcast doesn't bring in money directly, but it's impossible to outsource them since they require your appearance or your voice. That's OK. I learned that I should handle the writing for my clients. As a result, that means I have to outsource a much greater percentage of the work done outside my freelance writing business. But that benefits me in so many ways because I get to focus on the things that earn money or the things that only I can do.

When we merged over to new software, I didn't even hesitate to hire someone else to manage the migration and make sure everything was set up properly. It would have taken me 10 to 15 frustrating hours. Outsourcing it meant it took five. And there were no laptops being thrown at the wall or after-the-fact problems I couldn't sort out. It did cost me five

---

### Successfully Managing a Freelance Team

Bai-Leigh Chapman is a virtual assistant who runs her business with a few people behind the scenes. Even though she's only been in business online for the past two years, she realized she couldn't handle the broad variety of tasks often outsourced to VAs by herself. She also knew that she rocked marketing and bringing on clients, so she has subcontractors for social media, tech, and general admin to assist her in the business. She's in charge of strategy creation and initial startup, but the other team members help her with implementation and stats tracking. She's able to be front stage working the business and leveraging her reputation without having to handle every task that comes her way.

labor hours, but it saved me at least five more, plus the mental energy of doing it myself. In the end, it was a wise investment!

You cannot know where you want and need to go with your personal and business life until you complete an audit. Don't take a shortcut and guess—use at least one day's worth of data to point out your own weaknesses. Once you know where you can improve, it's much easier to make a plan for the future.

## —— CHAPTER SUMMARY POINTS ——

$   You need to outsource some tasks in your business, even if you do not hand off actual client work to subcontractors.

$   Knowing what you should be spending your time on is the first step to figuring out what to outsource.

### *Resources Mentioned in This Chapter*

$   Tasks Completed by VAs, Handout #9

# screening, training, and working with outsourced support

N ow that you've decided to find someone to help you with the tasks outside your zone of genius, it's time to dive a bit more into what that process looks like. Outsourcing means deciding which tasks and projects should be handled by someone else and regularly revisiting your business needs to decide if you should bring a task back in-house or if new tasks have emerged that require more hands on deck.

You already have the basic concept behind outsourcing in your back pocket. In this chapter, you'll learn how to find and hire the virtual assistants and other digital team members who are a good fit for your business.

## Attracting the Right Talent

The first step is posting a job description online. You should always include the following elements in any job ad for a virtual assistant or other outsourced support:

- $ The hours expected for the job, whether one-time, weekly, or monthly
- $ The software knowledge required to complete the tasks
- $ Your communication expectations, such as whether the person should live in a certain time zone
- $ How you prefer to give instructions and work with outsourced support
- $ Whether you have a certain budget in mind for this position

Check out the resources page on the website to view Handout #10, which contains the job description I used to hire my executive assistant and the Google Form that went with it. Having applicants fill out a Google Form tests how serious they are about the job and gives you a decent sense of whether they can follow instructions. (You can also view the job description in Figure 10–1 below.)

---

### Sample Job Description

*Now Hiring*: Exec Assistant/Digital Marketing Assistant

*Who's the client?* A multipassionate entrepreneur/author with a lot of projects going on at once. Works best with those who are self-directed go-getters. Niche: Work-at-home and freelancing.

*Looking For*: Six-month minimum role for an independent contractor; one-month trial period to start (paid)

*\*Please make a note early in your application if you are a veteran or military spouse.\**

**Your background/working style**

- Must be comfortable with intermittent communication during typical business hours (client is only available at night/early mornings/evenings to review things). I'm in Central time, by the way.

---

*Figure 10-1.* SAMPLE JOB DESCRIPTION

- Experience level required: new to intermediate.
- Has 10–15 hours per week to work on projects (sometimes one project might be more of a priority than others).
- Doesn't get swayed by helping to build in systems and processes.
- Wants to work with someone long term—not have 16 other clients at the same time. (No shade if that's you, that's just not a good fit for what I need.)
- Takes ownership of projects and mistakes (we all make them).
- Quick learner on software and has some awareness or interest in learning tools already.
- Not afraid to take initiative and learn new things (or speak up and say, "Hey, I actually hate this" or "we need to change this").
- Willing to work on launching a new nonprofit with a target audience of military spouses and veterans.

## Tasks

1. Outreach

   a. Coordinate guest posting outreach strategy for me to have 1-2 guest posts on other sites each month. Help with identifying ideal websites for me to guest post on.

   b. Connect with a few freelancers a day on LinkedIn to send them a customized message and add them to my FB group.

   c. Draft template email for weekly newsletter; schedule to send (tools to know: ConvertKit). Some light copywriting required.

   d. If you're interested in outreach, it's what I do full time and am happy to train you as a junior publicist!

   e. Make list of endorsers for my book; create template and arrange these emails to go out from my author Gmail.

2. Community support/social media

   a. Approve people for small FB group and manually add them to existing email sequence once per week.

*Figure 10-1.* SAMPLE JOB DESCRIPTION, continued

b. Schedule social media messages to go out through CoSchedule for new blogs (2–4 per month) and new podcast episodes (4 per month).

c. Manage the promotion of freebie/opt-in offers from my library through CoSchedule.

d. Add all old blogs/episodes into social media rotation on CoSchedule.

e. Pinterest management: schedule 1–2 times per month on Tailwind; add podcast episodes as needed with custom podcast graphic.

3. Back-end organization

a. Manage the creation/storage of freebies and keep book page resources updated.

b. Make a spreadsheet of all my media hits and previous podcast interviews

c. Manage booking, calendars, and Zoom scheduling for group meetings and masterminds. Ensure that all calendars seamlessly connect so no one double books and ensure that Calendly updates.

4. Book launch and marketing management support

a. Manage book launch for Oct. 2020 (book launch team, marketing, podcast pitching, etc. Training provided on this but bonus for someone who has worked with authors before). Primary goal: help me road map my marketing plan, target new podcasts, identify supporters/influencers. Project is managed on its own Trello board with clear action steps for the seven months before and the two months after the book launch (includes Amazon ads, Facebook ads, run by the client, monitored by you).

b. Manage book launch for self-published book (task-based projects, very similar to above). Book to come out in late 2020.

c. Track reviews and keep track of outreach in spreadsheets to prominent influencers in the freelance space.

d. Keep launch team on track with activities leading up to book launch day.

5. Other one-time projects

a. Organize updated information for speaking kit; proofread it and send to graphic designer.

*Figure 10-1.* SAMPLE JOB DESCRIPTION, continued

---

    b.  Create an affiliate page on my website for all the resources I love based on some direction I give.

    c.  Ensure each new posted blog or podcast episode has optimal SEO (minimum 2 inbound links, etc.).

    d.  Curate all old blogs to see what we need to delete and/or update.

    e.  Possibly make old blogs into Lumen5 videos; post on YouTube.

    f.  Outreach to podcast shows for me (I will train you on this).

    g.  Help me figure out a way to better filter email.

    h.  Revise my Upwork profiles for maximum searchability/greatest achievements.

6.  Podcast management

    a.  (Not audio editing or adding podcast to site, but show notes, social media image creation, and promotion.) Bonus points: suggest creative ideas for growing my listenership, sponsorships, etc.

    b.  Identify potential guests; collect information from them.

    c.  Post audio/video version to YouTube.

    d.  Communicate with guests (1–2 per month) about their show going live on the podcast. Provide them with the link and make sure they have graphics to share.

Software to know or ones you're willing to learn: Canva, CoSchedule, ConvertKit, Trello, Voxer, Tailwind, WordPress (not massive design, just content management/buttons, etc.).

---

*Figure 10-1.* **SAMPLE JOB DESCRIPTION,** continued

When posting your job description, refer to Handout #11 on the book's website for the best places to find a virtual assistant or freelancer to find some specific examples.

The very best place to look for outsourced support is through a personal recommendation from someone you trust, but this isn't always possible. Upwork is always a good starting point to find virtual assistants online. Similar freelance websites include Freelancer and Guru.

Using a tool like Google Forms or JotForms makes it easy to capture the information you need from your application. In Google Forms, you can export the information into a spreadsheet. Once I close down a job application, I go through the spreadsheet to decide which applicants I definitely will not be interviewing, which ones are a "maybe" if my first-choice selections don't work out, and my top candidates to ask for an interview. I use color-coding as I go to keep it simple: green for "definitely want to interview," yellow for "maybe if my green candidates fall through," and red for "this person is not a good fit."

### What to Look For in Applications

When screening the incoming applications, look for someone who ticks your most important boxes and identify where you are willing to adjust your expectations. For example, if they absolutely must know how to enter your potential clients into HubSpot CRM, look for someone who already knows how to use it. If a candidate has experience with the software you need but lives in the wrong time zone, perhaps that's an area you can compromise in.

Some qualifications will always be more important than others, so stay flexible. In my most recent round of hiring a subcontractor, I was bringing on an executive assistant. The person I hired was not the least expensive; however, she was by far the most qualified, so I adjusted my budget to start off with fewer hours per week so I could afford to hire her.

When evaluating potential candidates, consider the following:

$ Proficiency in tasks described in job ad
$ Overall interest in your personal brand (did they bother to look you up and comment on it?)
$ Their hourly rate and/or packages
$ The general personality style described in text

When looking for candidates to eliminate, I usually start with those who lack the right background or proficiency in the skills I need, followed by those whose rates are far too high and far too low.

### Interviewing Your Prospective VA

You wouldn't be hiring a VA if you weren't already busy. (Since a virtual assistant is the most common first hire for a scaling freelancer, we've used

## My Hiring Mistake: Not Hiring for Personality

Several years ago, I was in the market for an online business manager (OBM). I was creating a lot of courses, updating my website, and implementing opt-ins that required some tech savvy and an assistant with the ability to strategize. I quickly searched the internet and found someone who seemed like a good fit.

The testimonials were there. The list of skills and software knowledge was there. The pricing was high, but upfront. And here's where I made my biggest mistake: The candidate was working on retainer "as much as I needed" through the month. In theory, this sounded good. After all, if I were launching a new product one month and needed her for 40 hours, that would be covered by the retainer. It would be on me to make sure she had enough work on her plate.

If I had asked the right questions in the interview, I might have avoided the disaster that followed. Her business model included bringing on up to 12 "as much as needed" clients at a time. Often my tasks fell to the bottom of the pile and were completed late, done sloppily, or ignored altogether. When I brought her attention to it, she blamed me. She'd promise an update on Monday, and then I wouldn't hear from her for more than a week. When she did reach out, it was clear she spent no more than a half-hour rushing to produce something to show she'd worked on the tasks I had assigned to her.

It was a waste of money. The "projects" she completed were such a mess that I'd have been better off if she'd never touched my website at all.

Even though her work style was unlikely to be a fit for most people, the blame fell on me for how I conducted the hiring process. I didn't ask about communication style. I didn't ask how many clients she had or how many clients she hoped to work with at once. Instead, I wound up in a three-month contract that I ended early so I could hire someone else to fix all the messes she made.

But I learned from that mistake.

Another person I was considering for a content manager position passed the initial interview with flying colors. I checked her references (they loved her!), and her website and LinkedIn profile were full of the detail-oriented approach I was looking for. But my gut told me to do

---

### My Hiring Mistake: Not Hiring for Personality, continued

a second interview with my top two candidates, and that "shining star" had a total meltdown on the video call. I declined to hire her and tweaked my processes again to screen for issues earlier on.

There's a lot to be said for a VA's personality, too. If they prefer to receive written instructions but you don't have the time or any interest in doing that, they will constantly ask whether you can document in writing. While there's no clear metric to measure, a video call is your chance to see if you and the VA "get" each other. Once you start listening to your gut, the top candidates will emerge.

---

it as an example throughout this chapter.) So you might want to skip the interview process. Don't. Some candidates look great on paper but just don't have the personality to work well with you. Knowing this upfront helps you avoid having to let them go after a few weeks.

There's a lot more to hiring than the skills to do the tasks. It's about personality, communication style, and the candidate's intentions for their business. For example, you might not want to work with a VA who wants to start their own online course business in the future rather than help you build your freelance business. If they want to have as many clients as possible, that might not work for you if you want someone focused on you and a few other clients.

Depending on the depth of the job, I usually interview three to five people. If it's a one-time outsourcing project, you probably don't need to go that far, but if the hire will be client-facing, definitely speak to them on a quick phone or video interview.

Stuck on what to ask? Check out Handout #12 on the resources page on the website to learn more about interview questions that can help you reveal whether a candidate is the right person to work with you.

## How to Screen Test a Virtual Assistant

In this section, you'll learn more about using a test job or sample job to try out a new VA. A test job is a small example of the kind of work the candidate would do with you if hired that gives you a sense of their abilities and communication style.

I strongly recommend using both interviews and a test job when hiring a virtual assistant. Your application process will help you weed out unqualified applicants. Interviews can then help you determine which of the remaining candidates have the right personality and communication style to function well in the role you've defined.

But someone who makes a great impression in an interview might have trouble meeting deadlines or delivering the kind of quality work you need. The test job is your chance to verify that. I suggest testing two or three candidates because you might be surprised at who rises to the occasion and who falls short.

The following are elements of a strong test job:

$ Reflects at least some of the tasks you'd want the candidate doing on an ongoing basis
$ Has a clear deadline that gives the candidate four to seven days to complete the test job
$ Explains how the project is to be delivered to you
$ Includes a sample of what you do and do not want

If you're hoping to tackle a bigger project with your new virtual assistant or have an ongoing need, like social media scheduling, choose one small portion of that project to use for the test job.

To see a sample test job, check out Handout #13 on the resources page on the website.

Here are some other possible test jobs, depending on the kind of tasks you might want to outsource:

$ Outline a blog post for someone who will be helping with your own blog or client blogs
$ Research a specific topic to find five examples of something, when the bigger project involves finding 50 examples
$ Create one or two images for use on social media, based on your current website and branding

When it comes to payment, it's easiest to offer a flat rate for completion of the test job. The applicants coming in through Google

Forms or JotForms will offer a range of hourly rates if you ask, so you can determine a fair amount based on what seems to be the average rate and the technical expertise required for that project. Make sure that the instructions regarding the test job are very clear, including how you will pay them.

## How to Use Trial Periods to Your Advantage

A trial period is another way to vet a candidate without overcommitting. This is an opportunity to work with a new virtual assistant and decide whether you are compatible enough for a longer-term commitment. Even if you're inclined to hire them on a long-term basis, it never hurts to go with a trial period to start with. A trial can last a few days or a week for

---

### Case Study: Amanda

Amanda was in the market for a virtual assistant to help her with her content writing projects. She wanted a VA who could research keywords and outline blog posts for her, so that when Amanda was ready to write, she'd have everything she needed and could work quickly.

After we wrote and posted her job description, two applicants seemed to be the best fit. To decide between them, I encouraged her to assign a test job and pay both of them to do it.

The candidate who seemed like Amanda's top choice totally failed the test job. She never asked for more instructions or confirmed she'd be able to meet the deadline. The day the project was due, she completely flaked and didn't turn it in on time. When Amanda reached out to her to figure out what had happened, the VA was unresponsive. Amanda was shocked. The other candidate turned the project in on time, asked intelligent questions, and was easy to work with. It was an easy decision: The second candidate got the contract.

With test jobs, the cream generally rises to the top. The right person will see the potential in the test to gain a good client or even a long-term relationship and will make sure they knock it out of the park. If the candidate doesn't meet the deadline or follow instructions, it's a good indication they don't have the organizational skills to get their work done on time or the communication skills to ask the questions they need to ask to get the ball rolling with the project.

---

a smaller project, or run as long as a few weeks if the scope of the job is more involved.

Any virtual assistant worth their salt will easily rise to or exceed your expectations during this initial trial, whereas a person who lacks the necessary experience or has trouble following through will likely flake out in week two or three of a longer contract. While you will obviously do everything in your power to hire the right person for the job before hiring them, you cannot always avoid making mistakes. Sometimes the person who seems perfect on paper or even in the interview process is a nightmare in practice. It's far better to learn this during a two-week trial period than after you have been locked into a three-month or six-month contract.

> Look for the applicant who goes one step beyond what you've asked. That person has the interest and ability to stay ahead of you and offer assistance beyond just getting their tasks done.

Most virtual assistants who really want to work with you will see this trial period as their opportunity to shine. Those with some experience will also know that many clients have been burned before and will not take it personally.

Check out the sample test job in Handout #13 on the resources page on the website to get an idea of how much detail to provide your candidates.

## Giving Great Instructions

Most failed VA/freelancer relationships boil down to two factors: hiring the wrong person or giving poor instructions. Both of these problems are mostly avoidable, but remember: Giving great instructions might look different for you than it does for a VA. Your test job will reveal whether the VA understands the way you talk and provide details. If they ask 20 questions about your brief test job, they either don't understand how you think or you need to do a better job giving instructions. If you felt your project instructions were very clear, reconsider whether you're saving any time by hiring a person you have to go back and coach that frequently.

Use the tips from the test job on Handout #13 to make sure you've given clear instructions. Here are some additional tips that have worked really well for outlining processes the VA might need to follow again and again:

$ If the VA prefers written instructions, provide screenshots in a Google Doc they can also update on their end.

$ If the VA does well with video, consider providing a live training session through Zoom that you record and store for future reference, or make a video of yourself doing the process on a screen capture tool like Loom.

$ Ask the VA to help create standard operating procedures—as they note a new process, ask them to record it for future reference.

The more organized you can be in working with your VA, the easier it will be for them to get to work for you right away.

## Paying a Virtual Assistant

Much like other freelancers, you will find virtual assistants with pricing that ranges across the board. Look for someone who has the right mix in terms of experience, personality, and a rate that fits your budget. If you find someone you love but can't quite afford yet, consider adjusting their hours down for the first month. If they work on your projects for ten hours and end up saving you a lot of time, this can be increased to 15 hours. Sometimes it's far better to hire the right person at a slightly higher rate than someone cheaper who requires a lot more handholding on your part. You won't save any money that way.

### Hourly vs. Retainer or Project-Based: What's Right?

For tasks that could vary in terms of completion time, paying an hourly rate works well. Editors, for example, often charge by the hour for proofreading or editing a manuscript.

Most VAs offer scheduling and payment packages in one of three ways:

$ Blocks of hours that can be purchased as a package and used as needed

$ Hourly rates that are charged on an ongoing basis

$ Retainer packages that include either a certain number of hours, certain projects to be completed each month, or a hybrid model

With a block of hours, the VA has a set price for a package of 5, 10, 15, or some other amount of hours. This makes sense if your needs vary and you're not sure you'll need the same amount of their time every week. But make sure you read the fine print: Some VAs do not allow unused hours to roll over into the next month. With this method, payment is required upfront. Here are three examples of ways to pay VAs:

*Example*: I hired an OBM with a block of hours once, and she would tell me when she was getting close to using up the ten-hour package I'd purchased. I could then decide if I had more projects I wanted her to work on and needed to purchase another package.

With hourly rates charged on an ongoing basis, you will receive an invoice after the VA has completed work for you. If you have a smaller project where you don't think you'd use the bigger package or a block of hours, this method works best. It's often how people start working with a VA.

*Example*: When I hired a VA to help me with some keyword research, her job was to find 20 titles worth writing about. Since neither of us was sure exactly how long that might take, I hired her at a flat hourly rate and asked her to contact me if it ended up taking longer than a few hours. On a retainer model, you and the VA have agreed on a flat rate you'll pay every month for their services. The terms of your agreement might include a set number of hours or clear definitions of completed projects.

*Example*: Most of my VAs are on a retainer model now because we've worked together long enough that it's clear what they'll be doing for me each month. Andrew Sedillo, for example, manages my Teachers Pay Teachers online store. He uploads a few new lessons each month, responds to customer inquiries and reviews, and pins our lessons on Pinterest. Since his duties are so clearly defined and don't change from month to month, I can pay him a monthly retainer.

When I coach virtual assistants, I often discourage their use of hourly rates. Clients hate getting a surprise invoice for ten hours' worth of work when they expected it would only take four. This creates an awkward dynamic between client and VA, since the client feels they now need to micromanage the VA's time. But there's an easy solution for clients: When passing off a project to a VA, suggest a time estimate.

Here's a sample estimate I gave to my former content manager: "I'm thinking that adding four YouTube videos to the site per month and four blog posts on LinkedIn/my writing website will take around five hours. Does that sound right?"

Providing your expectations upfront also gives the VA a chance to push back and tell you when you've underscoped or overscoped the project, and it all but eliminates "surprise" billing. Tell your VA that if they start on a five-hour project and realize it's going to take longer, they should pause their work and run it past you before continuing. This simple process avoids any awkwardness and ensures their invoices will be in line with what you approved. (If you're paying on retainer or buying blocks of hours, it's still a good idea to ask the VA if your time estimate is on track.)

Once you've contracted with a virtual assistant on a longer-term basis, some VAs have their own ways they prefer to be paid, so make sure those gel with your preferred process. Ask them during the interview how they typically bill their clients. If you end up bringing on more than a few people onto your team, it's time to set up a formal invoicing structure. I accept invoices on an ongoing basis, but I only process them through a specific email address once every two weeks. For an invoice to be paid, it must be received by the close of business the Wednesday of that week so I can verify it's accurate. Invoices received late or with errors get bumped to the following invoice payment period.

Since a VA is a freelancer just like you, check the contract carefully for late fees or other terms that could impact you. Paying your independent contractors on time makes them much more likely to work with you again. Model positive payment habits, since that's the way you'd want to be treated, too.

## Onboarding a VA

Getting ready to work with your new VA means thinking carefully about how you'll give them the right tools and training they need to succeed with you. This is much like the process you go through when onboarding your new freelance clients: a chance to train, ask questions, and gain access to the tools, sites, or guidelines they need.

## Signing a Contract

Before your new virtual assistant starts work, you may want to ask them to sign a nondisclosure agreement (NDA) or contract with you. Often the VA will provide you with their own contract to protect their interests and clarify the working relationship. Carefully review any clauses that explain how much notice you need to give them before terminating the working relationship; most VAs will be willing to negotiate this. You should avoid having to work together awkwardly for extremely long periods after giving notice, like one month.

## Training Your VA

The level of training required for a virtual assistant is directly correlated to the complexity of the tasks or the volume of work you want them to complete.

Onboarding an online business manager who will be responsible for most of the operations in your business could take several weeks or even a month, whereas bringing on a new research virtual assistant working only a few hours a week might take a week or less. You can reflect back on your own freelance background when deciding how much training is appropriate. There is a fine balance between providing enough details to allow them to succeed and overwhelming them with too much information and coming across as a micromanager.

Give them opportunities to ask questions and tell you whether they feel they have received enough training. Creating a training schedule can be very helpful for explaining your expectations and allowing a virtual assistant to absorb your processes a little at a time.

When you hire your first virtual assistant, ask them to be actively engaged in the process of creating standard operating procedures and instructions along with you. You don't need to spend days or weeks creating an operations manual; the virtual assistant can fill in a loose outline as they go through the training process. This makes it more personal for them and thus more likely to be remembered.

## *Setting Up Communication Tools with a VA*

Determine your preferred method of communication with your new virtual assistant as soon as possible. While you might not need a separate project management tool such as Trello for just one virtual assistant, it can be useful if you need to keep track of more than three people. Project management software becomes the one-stop hub for everyone to ask questions, upload documents and other materials for review, and track deadlines. If at all possible, get these processes out of your email inbox as soon as you can. Even a Google spreadsheet tracking deadlines and ongoing processes is better than trying to keep track of projects via email, where there is a lot of opportunity for things to slip through the cracks.

Make sure your VA knows the best way to get in touch with you, and if you notice problems early in the relationship, respond to them appropriately. If you notice that your VA is getting stuck and interrupting you often, start scheduling a twice-a-week meeting where the VA gets a chance to ask their questions without disrupting your work.

Hiring a VA who clicks with your communication style from the outset will make this transition much easier. If you love giving verbal instructions but your VA needs written step-by-step directions, this will be a challenge again and again.

## *Setting Up Your VA with the Right Tools, Passwords, Etc.*

Just like automating a good portion of your client onboarding process, social media, and other marketing methods can be beneficial for growing your freelance business, so too can having established ways to pass on information to your virtual assistant. You should not store any of these passwords inside an email or an online document that could be accessed by outside parties.

Thankfully, there are many free tools available today that allow you to share necessary passwords with a virtual assistant and just as easily revoke that access in the future if they are no longer part of your business. Two favorites are 1Password and LastPass. Create folders inside these accounts for information often shared with team members, such as social media, your website, or even your email account. This makes it easy to go back and delete their access in the future if they are ever terminated or leave on their own.

The last things you should outsource to a VA are anything directly related to payment or personal details. Giving them free access to your Amazon account where your credit card information is stored is something you wait to do until they have proved trustworthy. Likewise, adding them to your accounting or invoicing systems, where they could see how much you charge and make within the business, should be postponed until you have established trust or a need for them to see that level of information.

When it comes to a virtual assistant hire, start small. A person who knocks it out of the park managing your website could be a perfect fit for expanded trust and responsibility, whereas someone who couldn't complete basic tasks should not be given more password access.

## Tips for Outsourcing Parts of Your Process

If you started to break down your processes in Chapter 8, you already know the general steps that each project will go through (with some room for customization as needed). Even if you're the one completing the actual client work and don't want to offload that onto a subcontractor, there is some room for you to hand off pieces of the process to someone else. Here are some examples of how you can continue to own the creation and client production process while still freeing yourself of unnecessary tasks:

$ A website designer might ask a virtual assistant to create and implement an onboarding sequence and series of questions to ask clients. This could save the designer a few hours every time.

$ A freelance writer might outsource topic and keyword selection and identification of resources or proofreading once the piece is complete.

$ Any freelancer might consider training someone to identify potential prospects to send pitches to or having someone set up sales calls within their calendar.

## Outsourcing in Your Personal Life

Outsourcing is not just limited to your business. A successful freelancer with a commitment to scaling will also leverage at-home outsourcing wherever possible. What this looks like for you vs. another freelancer might vary, but it could include meal preparation, dog walking, lawn mowing, laundry, cleaning, or organization.

A key mindset issue for a scaling business owner relates back to the idea that since you *can* do these tasks, you *should* do them. It's true—if you own a lawn mower, you could mow your lawn. But whether it's the best use of your time is another issue.

Focusing on your zone of genius allows you to get the most out of your working hours, but it also helps prevent you from edging into the burnout zone with your home responsibilities. Women are most likely to fall into this trap, although anyone who has a lot of home chores should consider what they can take off their plate.

If outsourcing your personal tasks to someone else allows you to get more work done, get some much needed downtime, or spend more time with your family, consider it a win.

## What to Do If Your Virtual Assistant Doesn't Work Out

One of the toughest issues you face in hiring a virtual assistant is what to do when things don't work. You might have done all the proper legwork in posting a job description, screening candidates, and hiring the person who seemed like the best fit. But what happens if the relationship, for one reason or another, doesn't pan out?

Unfortunately, this is one of the most challenging aspects of running a freelance business because you are likely to encounter it at some point. Even with the best intentions and the best hiring processes in place, you can still make a mistake, and a person who seemed to be a perfect fit on paper and during the interview process doesn't mesh well with you. You might discover this during the trial period or after you have worked with them for some time.

### When to Give Someone a Second Chance

When you first realize that your VA isn't living up to your expectations, keep in mind that it could be due to a mistake on your end. Perhaps you weren't clear enough when giving them directions, or maybe they need further training before they can really shine. Regardless, you should always give them an opportunity to improve their performance.

The first thing you need to do when there are errors and issues inside your business is evaluate the situation and determine whether they can be fixed. Have a conversation with them before you jump to conclusions; there's a good chance you'll learn whether they are aware of their problems and how willing they are to correct them. If they don't seem to think anything is wrong or are combative, this may be a sign that you don't need to invest any more of your time or energy in trying to bring them up to speed. It might be better to simply end the contract and move on.

## Outline Where Expectations Were Missed

Most of the time, however, they will want to work with you to correct any problems. In that case, you need to be as clear as possible when addressing concerns with your VA. Explain where you thought they would be and what happened instead. If your primary concern is that they have not been meeting deadlines, for example, express this directly.

If there has been a miscommunication over instructions, circle back, ask what happened, and determine whether they feel further training would benefit them. Always give them an opportunity to ask questions and provide their own feedback about the issue. The way in which they respond to challenges can tell you a lot about how they run their business and whether you will be able to fix this situation.

## Outline a Plan for Improvement

It is not enough to say that you think expectations have been missed and that you hope things improve in the future. Determine how you can help them move forward and what details you can provide to help them be more effective. The solution might not always be obvious, which is why you should always schedule to have the conversation first.

Outlining a strategic plan for improvement is important. If they are closely involved in your business, your strategic improvement plan might include 30 days of action before holding a meeting to circle back. Once you schedule this circle back meeting, the virtual assistant will have a clear metric to work toward and will understand that they will be reevaluated at that point.

While many virtual assistants are extremely professional and understand the critical role they play in your business, some might not realize that they will be expected to meet regular deadlines and share their progress in these evaluation meetings. Giving this information to your VAs upfront can clear up any confusion on this front.

## How and When to Fire a VA

When you know it's time to let someone go, do so professionally. Advise them of the last date you'll be needing their support, write up a quick list of what, if anything, they need to finish before departing, and set a calendar reminder for yourself to revoke their password access. If you know you'll need someone to replace them, restart the interview process so you can begin talking to candidates as soon as possible. Usually you don't need to go into detail about why the relationship is ending unless the VA asks for clarification or feedback. Remaining firm and clear will make it easier for you to cut ties and start fresh with someone else.

And don't be discouraged if it doesn't work out with one VA. If at first you don't succeed, outsource again. Review the situation and decide whether you learned anything that you could use to improve your process.

Every single freelancer I know has hired the wrong VA or other subcontractor at least once. Don't let this be an excuse to slip back into your old habits, where you do all the work by yourself. The right person is out there; keep looking and refining your processes or hire a coach to help you get your hiring project off the ground.

## —— CHAPTER SUMMARY POINTS ——

$ Every freelancer can benefit from some kind of outsourcing in their business so they can work as the CEO and in their zone of genius instead.

$ Deciding to hire someone requires you to think about what you write in the job description and how you manage the interview and onboarding process.

$ Build systems and expectations with your new virtual assistant from the beginning.

$ Before letting a VA go, attempt to fix things. If you have to part ways, do so professionally.

## *Resources Mentioned in This Chapter*

$ Job Description and Google Form Example, Handout #10

$ Best Places to Find a Virtual Assistant, Handout #11

$ Interview Questions to Ask Your VA, Handout #12

$ Test Job Example, Handout #13

# your future-oriented business

recently gave a talk at my undergraduate alma mater titled "The Power of the Pivot." It was all about my strategies to grow and move into new fields and projects and how to know when the time was right to pivot. The room was packed with students, which surprised me. How could college students know they needed to pivot already when they hadn't yet had their first job? It was a wakeup call for me: Everyone is interested in growing, evolving, and becoming the best version of themselves. That includes the person who shows up every day in your professional life as well as the hobbies and goals you pursue outside your career.

Even though the title of this chapter is "Your Future-Oriented Business," it could just as easily be "Be a Future-Oriented Person." You might decide to change up your business next month or six months from now. This chapter is designed to help you stay adaptable and know when it's time to grow and fold in new projects.

Freelancing completely online didn't even exist 20 years ago, and so many new tools and approaches have evolved since then. With the quick pace of technology, you can anticipate needing to revisit and retool your business as time goes on. Furthermore, many more freelancers are expected to enter the market in the next few decades, which means it's essential to stay competitive by always looking to the future.

The frenetic pace at which we do business is both a positive and a negative for freelancers looking to scale. On the one hand, it's easier than ever to find and connect with clients. We have access to other freelancers and software that help us work faster. But many of the tools we use today could look very different in a few years—or might be replaced by something else entirely. This is why you must be mindful of the fact that you can use this fast pace to your advantage while always being ready to adapt and change as needed.

We have already mentioned the importance of being able to adapt and define new territory, and we're going to reemphasize it here, especially as it relates to upskilling. As freelance writer Cyn Balog noted, downtimes in your freelance business shouldn't cause you too much stress since they're a great opportunity for you to learn new skills. She said, "Summers are notoriously slow in my business. When you find you aren't so busy, that's the time to invest in your business. Redo your website. Work on financials. Find ways to do things faster and more efficiently. Attend a class."

In this chapter, you'll learn more about staying ahead of trends, building in other components to your business, and protecting yourself from common pitfalls encountered when growing or sustaining a six-figure freelance business.

## The Freelancer's Introduction to Upskilling

Upskilling is the process by which employees of a business learn new skills to enhance the performance of their job. In a traditional employment situation, your boss might require you to attend some form of regular training. In your six-figure freelance business, you're that boss. So don't hesitate to assign yourself training that will help you grow and scale your business.

While there are certainly plenty of employees who might suggest learning something new, freelancers are more likely to see the value in upskilling, even on their own dime. It puts you in a great position to explore new services, charge higher rates, and be ready to adapt if your previous service offering undergoes big changes.

Upskilling isn't just about recognizing the fast pace of technology or anticipating that you might want to switch jobs in the future. It's a necessity, as explained by the World Economic Forum's 2018 "The Future of Jobs" report: At least 54 percent of the work force around the globe will need some form of upskilling or reskilling in years to come. This is because of the fast past of technology and new software tools or methods that are developed and become more popular. Consider jobs such as "Facebook ads strategist" that didn't exist ten years ago; it was likely digital marketing experts, writers, other ad strategists, and other kinds of freelancers that started learning how to run Facebook ads. Freelancers are more likely than employees to look for opportunities to learn and grow, including through videos, courses, podcasts, and books. The Upwork "Freelancing in America" study from 2019 found that 54 percent of freelancers had upskilled in some way in the six months before the study, compared with only 40 percent of nonfreelancers.

> "Never stop learning! Every day I learn something new that I'm able to apply to my business. The day you stop learning is the day you will no longer grow."
>
> –Bai-Leigh Chapman, freelance virtual assistant

These freelancers recognize the fast pace of technology and its constant shifts, but also the fact that new software, methods of working, and marketing options are emerging all the time. It's likely that new opportunities will continue to emerge in the next few years as well, and freelancers will be there to take advantage of them.

## *Upskill to Create a New Niche*

We freelancers are in the business of selling ourselves all the time, so we get asked plenty of questions about things like current issues in our industry and the state of digital marketing. That means we're more likely to hear about emerging trends before they hit the mainstream. For example, as an SEO content writer, a few clients asked me questions about how I thought voice search marketing and voice assistant tools might change the way people use search engines and how those search engines match results. It was great food for thought that led me down a rabbit hole of research in an effort to answer the questions, "Do I need to change my process? Do I need to learn some new tools so I don't miss out on this trend and so my work remains accurate and relevant?" I signed up for newsletters about new technology and studies around the concept of voice search so that I can continue to track how it might influence my content offerings.

Or consider Angela, a virtual assistant who had been doing mostly transcription work for legal and medical clients. She worked steadily in this field until around 2010, when she noticed a twofold trend. First, more transcriptionists who spoke English as a second language were now setting up virtual businesses in their home countries, where the cost of living was much lower. This meant she was suddenly competing for clients with other freelancers who were charging much lower rates than she could. In addition, companies like Rev.com and Otter.ai were leveraging big teams or artificial intelligence to make transcription easier, cheaper, and faster for companies of all sizes.

> "Invest in yourself by purchasing online courses, tutorials, seminars, or mastermind groups. The knowledge you receive from these is invaluable. Learning from others what has already been proven to work is the easiest way to become successful."
>
> –Derek Jacobson,
> freelance SEO expert

Angela saw the coming trends and knew she had to evolve. So she added another skill set to her arsenal: podcast support. Under that umbrella, she offered strategy sessions (since many of her previous transcription clients were podcasters) on how to start and grow a podcast, transcription and custom show notes, social media graphics, guest booking, and posting shows to the podcaster's website. This combated the automation and overseas outsourcing in her industry while broadening her skill set.

This was a really smart move because it also shifted Angela from a provider of basic services to a provider of premium services. Her clients were busy, and most of them were happy to hand off the entire podcast production process, apart from recording and editing the episodes, directly to her. This concierge-level service meant she could charge more, too. Her basic rate went from $35 per audio hour to $1,000 per month for podcast support. Many of her clients bought at above the basic package level, too, so she was able to leave her transcription-only clients behind. (They were also happy, because they turned to her competitors and got a basic price and fast experience for the one limited service they really needed.)

Angela was able to spot the trends and realize she had to evolve because she spent time working on her business as well as in it. She read books, listened to podcasts, and carefully monitored the data on her pitching, marketing, and conversion. She also took note of increasing comments from clients like "Wow, that seems expensive. Rev charges less and has a four-hour turnaround."

Like Angela, the more attuned you can be to coming changes and concerns, the easier it will be to start folding in new structures, systems, and offerings before it becomes urgent that you do so. It's possible Angela would have been able to compete for another few years, as Rev and overseas transcriptionists slowly chipped away at her earnings. But eventually she would have been forced to adapt or close her business. She decided instead to go ahead and evolve into a high-level service provider with a different set of clients. And she knows that if someone develops AI that can duplicate her current podcast production services, she'll either have to learn how to work with it or evolve yet again.

## Top Tools for Upskilling

Thanks to technology and the impact of content marketing, there are tools, lessons, courses, and training just about everywhere. There's a solution for every skill level and budget. Here are some of the best ways to build regular upskilling into your business.

### Online Videos and Courses

Watching someone else who has mastered a skill or a piece of software is a very valuable way to speed up how quickly you can learn something. It can cut through a lot of the confusion of written instructions, since you can watch exactly what someone is doing and learn from their experience. There are many free and paid courses and videos available on the internet.

### Podcasts

If you're busy working in your business instead of on it, podcasts are an excellent way to start incorporating new ideas and upskilling without much effort. Podcasts are audio only, making them perfect for listening to during a workout, while doing chores, taking the dog for a walk, or running errands in the car. Most podcasts are produced weekly, so the information in the episodes is usually timely. Since podcasts take time and money to produce, most people who make them have regular revenue streams so they can test and report back on new trends and ideas. Interview-style shows often feature modern thought leaders and innovators who can pique your interest about new concepts.

To get started with podcasts, check out iTunes on your computer and start searching for terms that describe your industry or online marketing/ service businesses. There are also many mobile apps that allow you to subscribe to your favorite podcasts whether you use an iPhone or an Android; search the applications store to find one you like. You can also search for people you follow and see what podcasts they have been interviewed on.

### Books

Books in electronic, audio, or print versions lay out business strategies and interesting topics. One of the potential downsides with books is that due to the long time between when they're written and printed and the limited options for revising them, those focused on specific technologies tend to go out of date fairly quickly. Check the most recent date the book was published or updated to verify accuracy.

Books are a great starting point, however, when you want to learn about a new topic and want to see the big picture. Since books tend to be much less expensive than an online course, they're a good way to see if there's enough demand on the client side and interest on your end before fully committing. For that reason, books are my first choice when I'm exploring a new subject area.

### Following Thought Leaders on LinkedIn

LinkedIn is an excellent tool for freelancers that we discussed in Chapter 5. It's also the main social media platform where people do business and share their professional opinions about trends and technology. That makes it an excellent place to connect with people you admire who are at the cutting edge of marketing. Following these thought leaders on LinkedIn gives you a chance to see their opinions and predictions in real time.

### Google Alerts

While not a foolproof way to ensure you get all the right content delivered to your email inbox, Google Alerts allows you to set up a stream of incoming emails based on relevant news articles and blogs on a topic with a keyword you define.

Upskilling and learning new technology will help position you better as a freelancer, but it is equally important for when you decide that you might want to change the primary drive of your business. Plenty of freelancers explore new passions and use them to expand from their initial skill set, and someday you might have to pivot from your core offerings that have worked up until now. Upskilling will help you prepare for that moment.

## The Freelancer's Guide to Pivoting

Freelancing is great. But doing whatever you do now might not be the right job forever, and there's nothing wrong with that. Give yourself permission to play and have new experiences when you're considering opportunities to learn.

Along the way, you might test the waters with many ideas that seem to go nowhere at first, but can still have value in the long term. I played with many ideas on the route to evolving my business. It looked something like this:

*Years 1 to 3 of my business.* Deliver freelance writing services in the form of blog posts and other web content to marketing agencies and law firms. Get invited to work as a digital project manager for Fortune 500 company; do so on a freelance basis to test it out.

*Year 3+.* Start experimenting with creating online courses to help freelancers manage their businesses more effectively. Investigate high-end coaching offers; decide it's not a good fit for me or my audience. Realize that courses have a lot of expenses involved in managing them; adjust expectations for course earnings. Experiment with outsourcing my client work and administrative/marketing tasks. Decide to handle client work myself but rely heavily on outsourcing administrative tasks.

*Year 4+.* Start experimenting with Fulfillment by Amazon (FBA), YouTube, and podcasting. Decide to only keep up with podcasting due to higher returns and better connection with my audience. Investigate what it takes to write/publish a book and do TEDx talks.

*Year 5+.* Start experimenting with one-on-one coaching supplemented by courses. Notice results are much better; build in accountability to all course offerings. Evaluate passive income streams and develop two of them.

*Year 6+.* Meet with public speaking coach and decide it's not a full-time fit; adjust expectations to four or five speaking gigs per year.

While this is just a big-picture view, it's a helpful summary to demonstrate that in freelancing, business continuously evolves. New opportunities emerge all the time, and something you thought you might love or expected to be easy could turn out to be another experience altogether, while something that seemed initially unpromising could end up being a central part of your business. Giving yourself space to test new things and then adjust or eliminate them as needed is vital. Your pivot can be based on personal preference, new connections or opportunities that come your way, or, like Angela's experience, increasing evidence that your current way of doing business isn't viable.

You can also pivot by raising your rates, offering new services in your existing freelance business, leveraging your freelance experience into a full-time job, or deciding that a non-freelance hobby, project, or side hustle is more appealing than working as a freelancer. But if you're starting to get burned out on your current freelance gig, one of the best ways to pivot is to look into sources of passive income.

## The Freelancer's Introduction to Passive Income

As you pivot, one of your chief concerns about your freelance business model is that you have to expend a lot of time and energy on projects that bring in money once. This is why passive income channels appeal to freelance business owners as a form of complementary revenue or a replacement for business revenue.

The term "passive income" is a bit misleading, because there are few projects that require little to no work. Almost every form of alternative income will require at least a little work to get started and some ongoing maintenance. That said, typical passive income projects require less work than completing a standard freelance project from beginning to end. As a freelancer looking to level up your business, diversifying your income is beyond smart—it might be essential. While plenty of freelancers do really well completing one-time projects, their ability to earn money is entirely dependent on their own work. That means that going on vacation or getting sick can throw a wrench into everything and degrade their income in a big way.

There are so many forms of passive income available to you, but to get your creative juices flowing, here are some ways I have made money outside my regular freelance services:

$ Books like the one you're reading right now!
$ Coaching other freelancers
$ Selling online courses on Teachable, Udemy, and Skillshare
$ Selling my old lesson plans on Teachers Pay Teachers

$ Using my copywriting skills to rewrite resumes and community service statements for Miss America state pageant winners

$ Affiliate programs where I get paid when someone buys a product I recommend

You are not limited to these ideas. In fact, here are some other ways freelancers can explore alternative income streams:

$ Rental properties

$ Investing

$ Building a following for their blog and selling ads

$ Starting a podcast and selling sponsorship spots

$ Starting an online store that sells printables

There are also plenty of ways to add new income streams that aren't passive. For example, when I launch a new course, I have to put in work to create it, record it, and promote it. But when I've been inspired to do it and feel like I can really help someone through the course, the money from the course sales is a good indication that I might be able to turn it into a passive income stream in the future. I know freelancers who have stepped way outside their comfort zone to dabble in completely unrelated projects, like trying voiceover work, going on acting auditions, selling quilts, and creating custom paintings. It might not be their main source of income, but it's a way to diversify while giving them a break from their usual freelance work. Having a creative outlet or something new to explore can even make you more productive in your freelance business.

The important thing is that you should feel excited about whatever income stream you're adding in. It should be something that lights you up.

For more information about passive income, I strongly recommend these two books, *Passive Income, Aggressive Retirement* (Money Honey, 2019) and *Money Honey* (CreateSpace, 2017), by Rachel Richards, the queen of income streams. Rachel appeared on my podcast and shared some excellent tips for getting started with passive income projects. She scaled her passive income to more than $10,000 per month, and she and her husband were able to "retire" much earlier than most people.

## Shiny Object Syndrome or Multipassionate?

Entrepreneurs often disagree about whether you should pursue all your passions or stay laser-focused on your business. I think the ideal strategy falls somewhere in between. If an idea keeps popping into your head, there's probably a reason for it. That's a bread crumb you should consider following. But if you change your mind every day about whom you want to serve and how you want to do it, the result is chaos.

The happy medium is streamlining the systems in your business as much as possible to free up time to pursue your other passions. There's no reason you can't have a side business or even just a nonmonetized hobby you enjoy. Filling every waking hour with the pressure of business or making each of your hobbies into a revenue stream is a recipe for burnout.

This is the way I like to add in new ideas: one at a time, a little at a time. When I relaunched my podcast, I spent two months making that my core project. That way I could discover if I had the stamina to stick with it long term and ensure I had the time to build out systems and processes for it so I could outsource as much of the work as possible. It was my way to test whether I was serious about it. Likewise, when I started sharing free videos on YouTube, I waited a few weeks before testing any other marketing strategies so I could get a clear picture of whether I enjoyed it, whether making these videos moved the needle at all, and whether I should fold it in as an ongoing process or project. I ended up sticking with the podcast, but I left YouTube behind.

If an idea keeps nagging at you or you're getting signs from the universe that it's worth pursuing, by all means pursue it. Put some time on your calendar to think it over and talk it out with someone. Set up a few networking meetings and listen to some new podcasts about the topic. If it's been a few days or weeks and you're more hooked than ever, follow your passion.

Some people say "shiny object syndrome" isn't a thing. It is, but it's often misconstrued. Shiny object syndrome is more often related to what we see someone else doing, leading us into a vicious cycle of thinking that we're falling behind and need to do that, too. Here are some examples:

$ I just heard Christina got three clients on Twitter this week. I should try marketing on Twitter because she had success there.

$ I feel guilty that Tom blogs three times a week. I barely manage to publish one. I guess I should start writing three blogs a week.

$ Everyone is starting a podcast these days. I guess I should, too.

Do you see the common thread here? These aren't passions—they're guilt over what you think you *should* do. That's completely different from being an avid podcast listener and realizing that you'd love to host a 20-minute show because you light up inside thinking about the possibility.

## Getting Support for Your Growing and Evolving Business

Recognizing when you need support is crucial for growing a successful business. Living in a digital world, it's all too easy to feel isolated. And there's only so much you can talk about "funnels" and "onboarding" to your spouse before you drive them crazy.

One of the most common challenges freelancers face is isolation. In this section, you'll find some recommendations for building or joining communities—not only to help your business but also to improve your mental health.

As a companion to this section, please check out the resources page on the website to access Handout #14 to learn more about communities where you can meet and network with other freelancers. Whether it's a Facebook group, a few friends in your area who grab lunch once a month and talk business, or a more formal business support program, you can grow your company by leaps and bounds simply by being inspired and held accountable by others.

### Mastermind Groups

Mastermind groups allow you to connect with peers about common challenges and questions. They're often more affordable than one-on-one coaching because the phone calls or support aspects of a mastermind are held as a group. You should still get access to a business coach, but you are also expected to actively participate in helping other people in the group, in addition to asking your own questions.

Masterminds work really well if you get empowered rather than distracted by hearing other people work through their business challenges and share their wins. Usually, these groups meet weekly in a virtual setting or over a coaching call. Mastermind groups are more expensive than buying a course or book, but they're not as costly as one-on-one coaching with the leader of the group.

### One-on-One Coaching

One-on-one coaching gives you the chance to work directly with a professional. With that comes more privacy and more personalized recommendations and accountability. However, coaching is more expensive because of this personal touch. If you'd prefer to have a coach focused only on your business and find that you don't thrive in a group environment, however, it might be a good option for you.

### Local Entrepreneur Groups

One of the best ways to connect with people when you're on a budget is by joining a local networking group. If you live in a city, it's easy to find other freelancers you can share ideas with. If you don't live in a city, look for a regional or virtual meetup for entrepreneurs.

Joining an entrepreneur group means that you'll meet people outside the freelancing world, but you'll often make excellent connections and meet business owners who have mastered a skill that's relevant to your freelancing business.

If you're hungry for more community in the freelance space, check out the list of online communities in Handout #14, available on the resources page on the website.

## Schedule Time for Working on the Business

Your business procedures and vision deserve your attention at least once per month. Many people refer to this as their "visioncasting" or "CEO day." This is when you take a look at all your numbers and decide what action steps, if any, need to be implemented.

Even if you're busy with client work, take the time to think about strategy, vision, and where you're at. It's so easy to get caught up in the day-to-day grunt work of prospecting, speaking to clients, completing projects, and getting paid. But if you never back away to look at the bigger picture, you'll miss the chance to improve systems and processes across the board.

A once-a-month vision day is, at minimum, a blocked-off morning with no scheduled calls or projects. It's even better if you can set aside a whole day and tell your team and your clients in advance that you won't be available. Get rid of distractions by using your autoresponder to inform people you're out of the office (by this point in the book, you should be an expert on that anyway!).

Gather data from the previous month to help chart your progress, such as revenue, number of pitches sent vs. those that converted, the average hours you've worked each week, the number of current clients, and your expenses.

During the vision day, ask yourself the following questions:

$ How do I feel about my business on a scale of 1 to 10? (If 10 is "I'm so in love with the work I do that my biggest challenge is pulling myself away from my business for other obligations or life" and 1 is "I'm exhausted and wouldn't care if I lost all my clients and projects tomorrow.")

$ Which clients are on the chopping block?

$ How do I feel about the amount of work I've put in this month?

$ If I had any big or side projects on tap this month, did I make progress on them? Or did I backburner things I really wanted to improve?

$ Have any clients given me feedback this month that I should use to update my marketing materials or, if it was constructive criticism, I could use to improve processes and quality?

$ Am I doing anything I shouldn't be doing? What tasks am I still handling that a CEO should not be responsible for?

$ If I have outsourced work to others, how is that process going?

$ How do I feel about the services I'm providing? Am I still excited to complete the work?

$ Are there any new services or passive income projects I'd like to consider adding?

For a printer-friendly worksheet to help you with this process each month, please check out the Vision Day Worksheet, Handout #15, on the resources page on the website.

As you grow and change your company, you might change, too. Investing in your success is also about creating the vision for the next version of your company. Consider brainstorming questions like:

$ How can I support myself and make time to explore my passions?
$ What is the best way to transition into new roles within my own company?
$ How often am I taking full days off?
$ When is my next vacation planned? What back-end systems do I need to build to support this?

## Be Mindful of Burnout

There is something absolutely liberating about growing your business and scaling it to the six-figure level. However, if you take on too much and overwhelm yourself, you could end up suffering from burnout.

Burnout can be a result of taking on too much, working with the wrong clients, refusing to outsource certain tasks in your business, feeling overwhelmed by or tired of working in your service area, feeling too isolated, and many other factors.

All too often, it hits you like a freight train. One day, you're just physically unable to work. You can't seem to get enough sleep. You dread answering your emails. You stop caring whether you miss deadlines or even have any clients. It can take weeks or months to dig out of a true burnout cycle with no other support systems in place. The key to avoiding it is to spot the signs of impending burnout earlier when a painful crash can still be prevented.

The initial warning signs of freelancer burnout include:

$ Fatigue
$ Turning in projects late
$ Not caring about client work anymore
$ Dreading waking up in the morning and going to work
$ Difficulty sleeping
$ Constant anxiety

$ Stomach pain or ulcers

$ Waking up earlier and staying up later every day to get things done

$ Wishing you could close shop on your entire business

During a busy period, it's easy to dismiss some of these symptoms as the cost of growing your business. But it's not sustainable long-term.

Freelancers are notoriously bad at taking days off and vacations. I urge you: schedule your vacations six months in advance and prepay for them. That way you're committed. I once had a coaching client whose dream was to take off the two weeks around Christmas. I told her to go into Google Calendar and block it off months in advance as her vacation time. Seeing it labeled as "Busy" in her calendar really helped her disconnect and decompress. Sometimes it's that easy! When you do your quarterly planning, set aside time in that process to schedule vacations and days off.

If you notice that you're headed rapidly toward burnout and don't feel you can successfully walk it back, more drastic measures like cutting your workload or passing off some clients to subcontractors may be necessary. Of course, consider additional support systems like therapy and doctor's appointments to help with the mental and physical impacts of burnout, which are real and debilitating.

Here are some general tips to help protect you against burnout:

$ Use your monthly vision days to check on your workload and determine if you need to hire more help for your growing company.

$ Schedule firm office hours and close your laptop and office door at the end of your workday. (I put office hours of 8 A.M. to 4 P.M. in my email signature, not just to let my clients know but also to hold myself accountable!)

$ Don't get in the habit of checking your emails or working on client projects seven days a week. Sometimes weekend or evening hours are necessary, but view them as a temporary situation and then bounce back into a more manageable schedule.

$ Reinforce your boundaries often. If you notice a client is pushing the limits, consider letting them go.

## It's Your Time

Throughout this book, you've been presented with all the stops on the road map to six figures. While your mileage may vary in how and when you get there, you have all the tools you need to scale your business.

In the first few chapters, you learned how to determine your six-figure launch point, discovered the importance of a regular mindset habit, evaluated or confirmed your choice of working as a solopreneur or agency owner, and recalibrated what it means to have high-dollar, high-value clients.

From there, you dove into the marketing, systems, and strategies you need for your business to grow on a strong foundation. You learned about how to make outsourcing work for you and when it's time to add alternative income streams.

You already have what it takes to be successful. With some fine-tuning, your journey to six figures is ready to kick off!

## —— CHAPTER SUMMARY POINTS ——

$ Recognize the importance of upskilling and always stay tuned into your industry and technology for opportunities to learn new things.

$ Since freelancing is often one project at a time, where you get paid once for the item you've created, fold in passive income and recurring income projects to diversify your finances.

$ Regularly take time to determine whether you're happy with your business—if not, consider eliminating, adding, or restructuring your schedule and your offers.

### Resources Mentioned in This Chapter

$ List of Online Communities for Freelancers, Handout #14

$ Vision Day Worksheet, Handout #15

# acknowledgments

I owe a huge debt of gratitude to a few people who made this book possible in the first place: Megan Close Zavala, who was instrumental in helping me brainstorm and workshop the idea and proposal; my agent, Leticia Gomez; and the team at Entrepreneur Press, especially Jennifer Dorsey.

To all the freelancers I have coached in the past two years, thank you for allowing me to help you grow your business. I am extremely thankful for the input of other six-figure freelancers who reviewed early chapter outlines, gave feedback, and contributed their tips throughout the book. That includes Ana Reisdorf, Elena Orovio, Cyn Balog, Karine Bengualid, Ana Gotter, Jason Resnick, Bai-Leigh Chapman, Nicole Rollender, Leighton Taylor, Katelyn Magnuson, Meagan Wright Hernandez, Melissa Froehlich, Derek

Jacobson, Jennifer Wisniewski, Danielle Oloko, Sarah Fox, Alexis Gilbert, and Seraine Page. The members of my advance reader team were critical support in helping to get this project outlined. You all made this a better book.

Thanks also goes to my mom, Carol Pennington, who has always been a supporter and believer. To my husband, John, thank you for always believing that my business, this book, and so much more were possible. This one's for you.

# about the author

Laura Briggs is empowering the freelance generation. Through her public speaking, coaching, and writing, she helps freelancers build the business of their dreams without sacrificing all their time, family, or sanity. Laura burned out as an inner city middle school teacher before becoming a solopreneur with a Google search for "how to become a freelance writer." She has worked for more than 350 clients around the world, including Microsoft, TrueCar, and the Mobile Marketing Association. Laura has delivered two TEDx talks on the power of the freelance economy to enable freedom and flexibility. She's also the author of *Start Your Own Freelance Writing Business* and the founder of Operation Freelance, a nonprofit organization that teaches vets and military spouses how to start and grow online service-based businesses.

Outside of writing and business, Laura enjoys time with her husband, John, and her fur children Tigg, Max, and Frank.

# index